The

Lamb Wins!

'A highly imaginative look into the only book in the Holy Bible with a blessing attached to anyone who even reads it! Richard's descriptions give a view on Revelation that can only be likened to a biblical projection on the screen of your mind.'

John R Green, Broadcasting Manager, UCB TV

The Lamb Wins!

A guided tour through the Book of Revelation

Richard Bewes

CHRISTIAN
FOCUS

The dot texture on the cover is Revelation 5:6 set in basic Braille.

Then I saw a Lamb, looking as if it had been slain, standing in the centre of the throne, encircled by the four living creatures and the elders. He had seven horns and seven eyes, which are the seven spirits of God sent out into the earth (**Rev. 5:6**).

In the same way that Braille is completely incoherent to everyone but those who are taught to read and understand it, Revelation is completely incoherent to everyone but those who the Holy Spirit has enlightened to understand it.

Unless otherwise indicated Scripture quotations are taken from the *Holy Bible, New International Version*. Copyright © 1973, 1978, 1984 by International Bible Society.Used by permission of Hodder & Stoughton Publishers, A member of the Hodder Headline Group. All rights reserved. "NIV" is a registered trademark of International Bible Society. UK trademark number 1448790.

Scripture quotations marked KJV are taken from the *King James Version*.

This book is dedicated to our next-door neighbour and
inspiring colleague and friend over many years, John Stott.

www.richardbewes.com

paperback ISBN 978-1-85792-597-5
epub ISBN 978-1-78191-245-4
mobi ISBN 978-1-78191-246-1

Published in 2000,
reprinted 2003, 2006, 2013 & 2017
by
Christian Focus Publications,
Geanies House, Fearn, Ross-shire,
IV20 1TW, Scotland
www.christianfocus.com

Cover design by Alister MacInnes

Printed by Bell & Bain, Glasgow

MIX
Paper from
responsible sources
FSC
www.fsc.org
FSC® C007785

Contents

PART FIVE
THE OVERTHROW OF EVIL

PART SIX
THE NEW ORDER

FOREWORD

Richard Bewes and I sat down for breakfast. We were attending a Congress in Lausanne, Switzerland. Before we could tackle the croissants and jam, the high-powered delegate at the same table asked whether we took a particular view (which he named) of scripture. We hesitated – the answer was neither yes nor no – but our polite answering was not good enough! With a scowl, the man moved to another table! So often, when we come to the Book of Revelation, we meet branded, over-confident and over-detailed views that make *us* want to get up and move to another book! Not so in this 'guided tour' by Richard Bewes.

Later that morning, we boarded a trolley-bus, carrying a portable tape recorder, and there on the bus recorded a radio interview with a saintly overseas bishop, who had dared his life in the translation of the scriptures and had lived the gospel in the tough frontiers of evangelism. Not for him the branded views – but an overflowing love for his Lord, for the gospel and for the scriptures. We felt more at home on the trolley-bus than at the breakfast table.

We are on the trolley-bus in this book. It is concerned with the living church on the streets of Bermondsey, Bangkok or Baltimore – with the Church in action and not cooped up in a theological retreat house. If the Bible is the book for today's Church (and it is), then the Book of Revelation should be a book for today's Church (and it is). My very dear friend, Richard Bewes, sweeps us through it with a touch that makes even the back streets seem important and yet keeps the strategic parts in perspective. So get aboard – and see Revelation as you've never seen it before!

Michael Baughen

INTRODUCTION

'If only I knew what to do with Revelation!' So declared Karl Barth, perhaps the greatest theologian of the twentieth century. No wonder you and I may feel a little timid about plunging into this last – and somewhat bewildering – book in the Bible.

But let us try! Granted there have been some controversial interpretations of this fascinating prophecy, we need not feel browbeaten into making heavy weather of it. It is the message of Christ to every generation of his followers.

The Lamb Wins. The simple three-line slogan was all that featured on the sign erected by the small Methodist church in Prague. It was November 27th, 1989 – the day that Communist domination came to an end in Czechoslovakia. Until then the harassed Christian community had been permitted no publicity at all; even the displayed title *Church* was forbidden on the outside of the building. Now the message was movingly evident to the passers-by: 'The Lamb Wins.' It was not that victory had *at last* arrived. The theology of the little poster was exactly right. Christ is *always* the winner. He was winning, even when the church seemed to lie crushed under the apparatus of totalitarian rule. Now at least it could be proclaimed!

I love the book of Revelation. I first attempted sharing my discoveries from it at two conferences arranged in East Africa some years ago. Now I hope that these pages will encourage Christian friends to explore the Revelation at whatever level seems desirable.

This is not a commentary, and it has not been written primarily for the theologian – though I shall be glad if fellow-preachers find anything useful here by way of outline or illustration. You may wish to use this book as bedtime reading, or as something to take away on holiday. There is another use, however.

There are thousands upon thousands of small Bible study groups coming into being all over the world. Perhaps you are a member of one; you may even lead one. A church or student body could well decide to hold a series of six studies at the group level, and tackle Revelation. If so, you may find that the six-part arrangement of this book will assist you. Suggested questions are given, every three chapters, to stimulate group discussion.

And may God inspire and equip us as we hear what the Spirit is saying to the Church of Jesus Christ.

RICHARD BEWES
Written at
All Souls Church,
Langham Place, London.

PART ONE

CHRIST IS WITH HIS CHURCH

'But all the endeavours of men, all the emperor's largesse and the propitiation of the gods, did not suffice to allay the scandal or banish the belief that the fire had been ordered. And so, to get rid of this rumour, Nero set up as the culprits and punished with the utmost refinement of cruelty a class hated for their abominations, who are commonly called Christians....

Besides being put to death they were made to serve as objects of amusement, they were clad in the hides of beasts and torn to death by dogs; others were crucified, others set on fire to serve to illuminate the night when daylight failed....'

Tacitus, the Roman historian
after the fire of Rome, AD 64

1

CRACKING THE CIPHER

There took place in New York last century the sale of a painting that had been lost for a hundred years. Entitled *Icebergs*, it had been painted by the nineteenth-century American artist Frederick Edwin Church. It finally turned up in a boys' home in Northenden, Manchester.

The painting was dirty. Workmen had placed ladders against it, and it had been used as a dartboard. One boy had added his own signature alongside that of the artist. But when it was sold at Sotheby's in New York, it fetched several million dollars.

An unusual event? Not entirely. It has happened before, with ancient papyri, with musical masterpieces, with porcelain, coins and books. It is, indeed, a book that we shall be considering in these pages. The book of Revelation has not been appreciated in recent years as it should. It has become strangely overlaid by the oddest assortment of views and interpretations! It has become the playground of the cults. Ordinary Christians have left it unread; turned off by the bizarre flights of fancy, by the mathematical labyrinths in which some of its readers appear to have become enmeshed.

It is worth a rediscovery.

You will not find in these pages a heavily detailed verse-by-verse commentary. There are plenty of such commentaries. Rather, we shall set out to establish some of the great landmarks in this amazing book of Revelation, to recapture the strength, the inspiration and – yes – the comfort of John's great Apocalypse.

Apocalypse? The word is from the Greek and means simply a 'revelation' or 'unveiling'. Things that would be normally hidden from us are made known in Apocalyptic writing – such as we find in the book of Daniel, or in the Revelation. *Apocalyptic writing takes you behind the scenes and reveals the unseen principles that affect history – and the future.* It brings hope during times of crisis; it shows the end from the beginning.

'How otherwise could the Bible end?' asked Fred Mitchell in his study *The Lamb upon His Throne* (Marshall, Morgan and Scott). 'Supposing it ended at the Epistle of Jude? Then all that we should see would be ungodly men in their ungodly deeds to which they are committed, and the saints committed to contending for the faith once for all delivered to them. The issue in such a case might appear to be in doubt; but no, the Bible is complete, for in the last Book we see the climax of all the redemptive purposes of God.'

> 'The revelation of Jesus Christ, which God gave him to show his servants what must soon take place. He made it known by sending his angel to his servant John' (Rev. 1:1).

John ... no other identification is needed! The beloved apostle, an old man now, writes down the message of the Revelation as it is given him. He is an exile, banished from Ephesus to the island of Patmos, 'on account of the word of God and the testimony of Jesus' (1:9). Patmos is one of a cluster of small islands off the coast of modern-day Turkey. They were ceded to Greece after the Second World War. There, on the little hill-covered island, eight miles by four, John saw out his final days. It was there, one Sunday, that he received from the risen and glorified Christ the prophecy that ultimately was to round off the books of the Bible.

Way back as a youth, I did 'logarithms' at school. I even passed a mathematics examination, but to this day I couldn't tell you what logarithms were *for*. The columns of figures were, to me, as confusing as they were indecipherable. Some people, on approaching John's prophecy, seem equally baffled. Is it a question of cracking a secret code? How do you interpret this amazing series of visions? A quick survey of some of the main interpretations will help us. If we can get it right *now*, we shall save ourselves endless confusions.

The Preterist Interpretation
Preterist – here is a technical term, derived from the Latin word *praeter* ('past'). The preterist view interprets the book of Revelation as referring mainly to the *past events* of John's day, in the last few years of the first century AD. The Emperor Domitian was on the throne of the Roman Empire; the persecutions of Nero's reign had already taken place. 'Babylon' is a code name for 'Rome'; and the prophecy is given to encourage the harassed Church of that time. A valid interpretation? Yes, of course; *but it cannot stand alone*. Does the book not have a direct bearing on the events of history that were shortly to unfold? Definitely! So maintain the supporters of another view.

The Historicist Interpretation
On this view, we are to see the great bulk of the book (once we are past the first three chapters) as a kind of panoramic view of world history, continuously unfolding. It is a *history written in advance* – although by now, historicists would maintain, most of the events related have taken place.

A credible interpretation? Ye-es. I hesitate! The weakness of the interpretation lies in the tendency of the historicists to identify sections of the prophecy with those events of history *familiar to them* – usually the history of western Europe. Is this helpful and relevant to Christians struggling in other eras and in other countries? Naturally we are going to find many familiar historical *patterns* appearing in this study, but we must be careful not to press our interpretation into a rigid and artificial framework.

The Futurist Interpretation

This has been, and still is, popular today. It is the view that, after the first three chapters, most of the Revelation is referring to the future events near the end of time, and that most of the prophecy has yet to be fulfilled. Certainly the attraction of this approach centres in the triumphant statement of the ultimate victory of God:

> 'The kingdom of the world has become the kingdom of our Lord and of his Christ, and he will reign for ever and ever' (11:15).

And yet is the futurist approach enough, taken alone? Surely a good deal of the prophecy *does* relate to the time of the Roman Empire at the time of John, and indeed to a wider canvas altogether.

The Idealist Interpretation

Some Bible students would say, 'Look, we may not understand all the symbols and imagery of the Revelation; let it be enough that it is wonderfully symbolic of the victory that lies at the heart of Christianity. Be encouraged, but don't worry too much about the details.' I can sympathize with this view, because the book of Revelation is certainly very encouraging with its message of triumph in the face of adversity. And yet, to be of genuine practical help, should not the imagery be anchored to real situations and concrete events?

We would surely welcome aspects of every one of these approaches! But is there a view that encompasses something of all four? I believe there is.

The Parallelist Interpretation
A friend of mine told me how he read the book of Revelation for the first time. He had no aids, no commentaries to guide him. He simply opened at chapter one, and began reading. After a while he said to himself, 'This doesn't read like a continuous sequence. The writer keeps going back on his tracks. He seems to stop, and then begin to cover virtually the same ground all over again. And yet … each time he resumes, it's almost as though he sees the same familiar picture through different coloured spectacles.' My friend read on. When he got to the end, he reflected. 'The book of Revelation is basically presenting *one* picture. With every new section a fresh facet, a new colour, is added until in the end I've got the complete picture. It's like the process that goes into the making up of a picture in a colour magazine. You start with one layer of colour, then put in the next; the blue, the red, the yellow – until in the end the whole thing is complete.'

When my friend told me of his discovery, I realized that, with no one telling him, he had been pursuing what Bible specialists call the *Resumptive* interpretation of the book. The same identical picture is being 'resumed' repeatedly, albeit from different angles and viewpoints. Others call it the *Parallelist Interpretation*. We are reading the sections one after another – *but they do not actually follow each other as a chronological sequence. They are parallel to each other*. Sometimes we are looking at the picture from the viewpoint of the Church. Sometimes it is a heavenly view that is projected. Sometimes the picture is coloured by the theme of judgment, sometimes by that of victory.

Always the same picture, the picture being ... what, precisely? It seems to be the whole of this Church age that is basically in view – the entire era stretching between Christ's first and second coming – the era in which John and his readers were living, the age in which you and I are situated. These visions are given to strengthen the Christian of every century against the day when his own world seems to go up in flames. We learn from this book of the patterns that we can expect history to reveal; we allow its throbbing message of conflict and ultimate triumph to colour our own distinctive Christian world-view; we learn to see the end from the beginning; we develop our own certain expectation of Christ's return and victory, and shape our lives and our service accordingly. The preterist, historicist, futurist and idealist views are all included.

It is time for us to examine this wonderful prophecy, and to share a little in what John experienced one Sunday, on lonely, hilly Patmos.

For your reading
Revelation 1:1-8.

2

DON'T BE AFRAID!

It was Sunday – 5th October to be precise. The young Ugandan school teacher was in a rebellious mood. He had stamped out of church earlier that day, enraged by the Christian message he had heard. The rest of the Sunday he had spent drinking. Just then a friend rode up on a bicycle, and spoke to him.

'When I was in church today, something happened to me. God has forgiven me the wrongs I have done. Jesus has become my Saviour!' Apologising for various misdeeds, the friend rode off into the village.

It was like a thunderclap to the school teacher. For his best friend to desert him in his rebellion – to change his mind about God and about Jesus Christ!... It was too much. Years later he told me of how the encounter on the road had opened his eyes.

'I made for my room. I was kneeling, seeking forgiveness, seeking restoration. I began to cry to God, and my eyes were opened to his love on the Cross. I realized that the death of Christ was because of me. Then it was as if the Lord said, "This is also how much I love *you*."

'I felt a tremendous liberation. I had been running away from God's love – and now this freedom! I jumped to my feet. I remember saying, "Lord, give me permission for one more week ... just one more week ... to live – and I will tell everyone I meet about this!"'

Festo Kivengere – for that was his name – rushed outside. A woman was passing by, a hundred yards away.

'Stop! Stop!' shouted the young man. 'Jesus Christ has come my way today!' The woman tossed her head and turned away. Drunk! And on a Sunday!

But it was the beginning of a new life for Festo Kivengere. Later he was to become a great evangelist in Africa, and a bishop in the Church of Uganda. Everything had become alive on that Sunday evening, when the vision of Christ crucified and alive for ever had come into focus.

Whether it comes through normal or super-normal channels, it is – ultimately – a vision, a concept of Christ himself, that gives power to New Testament Christianity. Take that away, and we are left with the dead bones of a dry morality, devoid of comfort, and powerless to change anything. But the book of Revelation reminds us that Christianity is full of comfort – and has power to change the world! As in Festo's case, it was a Sunday when John caught his glimpse of glory:

'Among the lampstands was someone "like a son of man".... His head and hair were white like wool, as white as snow, and his eyes were like blazing fire.... His face was like the sun shining in all its brilliance' (1:13-16).

Here, surely was a sight that John had never seen before – *or had he?* Wait a moment ... he had!

'After six days Jesus took Peter, James and John with him and led them up a high mountain, where they were all alone. There he was transfigured before them. His clothes became dazzling white, whiter than anyone in the world could bleach them ...' (Mark 9:2, 3).

Way back on that mount of Transfiguration, before the death and resurrection of Christ had taken place, the three disciples had been privileged with a preview of the Kingdom – in miniature. They witnessed something very like the vision that had confronted Daniel hundreds of years earlier, a vision closely associated with someone described as 'like a son of man' (Dan. 7:9-14). What did it all mean for the exiled apostle on Patmos?

Christ is speaking to his Church
'I knew it was Jesus,' said the young Arab. He had happened to be in Kuwait on the eve of the Gulf War in the early 1990s, when Christ spoke to him. A Middle East TV news reader, and a committed Muslim, the message came to him like a thunderbolt: 'Get up, and leave this city immediately – and follow me.'

The young journalist had had no Christian background, and no Bible ... but there was, he said, no mistaking the identity of his apprehender. This has often been so in the case of Muslim friends confronted by Jesus Christ, whether by a vision or by some inner revelation. There is no comeback, no puzzled exclamation – *Who's that?* They know, and they are never the same again.

On this occasion the young journalist obeyed the summons instantly. His adventures were many, and hazardous, but they led him ultimately to central London, where – because his face was known in the Middle East – he changed his name and began a new life as a follower of Christ. I was privileged to be involved in his baptism.

There is something about the voice, the words of Christ. Many are the times when we hear him speaking, indeed, through a preacher. The apostle Paul tells his readers in Ephesus that 'ye have heard him and have been taught by him'

(Eph. 4:21, KJV). In point of fact the Ephesians had been completely unacquainted with Christ in his earthly ministry. They had only heard preachers! No, says Paul, 'You heard *him*' – and the King James translation of the Greek New Testament is better than modern versions which wrongly render the Greek, 'You heard *of* him'.

There is no mistaking that Voice! Christ's words have travelled across many centuries from the Galilean lakeside, but they are as powerful and inspiring as ever!

'Fear not ...' Those luminous words, spoken by a carpenter-preacher in the hills and valleys of Galilee, came to John the exile on that memorable Sunday in Patmos. It may have been in some kind of dream-state that John received his vision and heard the reassuring words. They sounded to him like rushing water – but there was no mistaking their origin!

> 'Do not be afraid, I am the First and the Last. I am the Living One; I was dead, and behold I am alive for ever and ever! And I hold the keys of death and Hades' (1:17, 18).

The vision and the message were not only for John. They are for the whole Church of Jesus Christ. Historically, they were for 'the seven churches' named in verse 11. On a Bible map, you will see that these seven towns are in what we know as western Turkey, and that they are grouped in a half-circle, beginning with Ephesus on the south-west, then north, east and south again in a curving line, ending with Laodicea.

Presumably the prophecy was to be passed from one church to the next. The message was for all of them, even though – as chapters 2 and 3 show – each church was to receive one of these 'letters' from the Son of Man for itself. It is also significant that these seven towns were traditionally *postal* centres of the area. They would have been ideal sites for the circulation of the message to other churches. Through this Apocalypse, Christ is speaking to all of his Church.

Christ is staying with his Church

The vision was one of someone 'like a son of man' among seven golden lampstands. Verse 20 tells us that the lampstands represent the seven churches. The 'angels' (or messengers) of the seven churches may well have meant the ministers, the leaders.

Why 'son of man'? It was Jesus' favourite title for himself. Although it seems to speak of his humanity, in reality it is a pointer to his deity. The term is drawn from the book of Daniel, in which a son of man is portrayed as ruling an everlasting kingdom (Dan. 7:9-14). Jesus used the name in three ways: when speaking of his earthly ministry, his death, and his coming glory (Matt. 8:19, 20; 20:17-19; 24:30). Perhaps our Lord used the name because it carried no nationalistic associations during his ministry; it implied an identification with *man;* so it had both overtones of divinity and undertones of humanity.

It is this divine, glorified Christ who has promised his permanent presence to the Church he has called into being. 'Surely I will be with you always, to the very end of the age,' is his promise (Matt. 28:20). No other body or society on earth has such a promise. It is to the Church that Christ has pledged his living presence. A presence is always superior to a memory! A memory inevitably fades; not so a presence. Christ is staying with his Church – in person.

Christ is searching through his Church

John fell down at the sight of the glorified Christ. No wonder. The figure he saw was not clothed with Galilean homespun, but with the robes of a priest. The brightness hurt his eyes. Everything about the vision spoke of great strength combining with holiness and purity. The head, the feet, the voice – and those eyes like blazing fire! Nothing could remain hidden from them.

The Son of Man's messages to the seven churches would inspire and lift – but they would also challenge and rebuke. It is vital that the company of Christ's followers should be characterized by purity – for the truth's sake, for the world's sake, and for Christ's sake. If we cannot maintain a clear cutting edge, who will? Christ is searching through his Church, with a holy scrutiny.

Christ is strengthening his Church

Domitian was on the Roman imperial throne. Asia Minor was a quagmire of strange beliefs and idolatries. There were the barbaric hordes waiting in the wings for their cue to enter the stage of history. Everywhere the fear of death prevailed among thinking people.

Into this situation were projected the beliefs of the new Christian sect – founded on the unusually solid base of an historical figure ... a real man who had lived, worked and suffered – and not so many decades ago! *'Why should your God come and live on earth?'* asked the second-century pagan philosopher Celsus. *'Didn't he know what was going on there?'*

It would take a long time for the real truth to penetrate. There would be misunderstandings and killings. But there it was on the world scene, an insignificant cloud no bigger than a man's hand – the Christian Church ...

... and among the lampstands was someone 'like a son of man' ...

Here lay the secret of the new movement's strength. Every church is like a lampstand, with its offer of truth and light for a world in darkness. Ours would be an impossible task – an unattainable dream, or a back-breaking chore, were it not for our vision of Christ at the centre of all our life and service:

> A vision with a task makes a visionary;
> A task without a vision makes drudgery;
> But a task with a vision makes a missionary.

Our leader holds the keys of death and Hades (1:18); no one else. And whoever has the keys has the authority!

For your reading
Revelation 1:9-20.

3

LETTERS FROM HEAVEN

No one is quite sure whether it was 22nd or 23rd February. It all depends upon whether it was a leap year. An old man had been arrested in what is today the second largest city in Turkey, Izmir. It was somewhere around the year AD 155. The crime seemed trivial enough – involving a mere refusal to offer a little incense to the Roman emperor. The imperial authorities were tolerant enough; a citizen was free to worship any number of gods – provided the state ceremonies were observed first. There were gods by the thousand! *'It is easier to find a god than a mortal in this city,'* was the comment of a businessman at dinner, in that period.

What was intolerable was the claim that any deity might have unique lordship, to the exclusion of others! And this is where Polycarp, the old man, fell foul of the authorities in Smyrna.

The sheriff – and even his father Nicetes – tried to reason with him as they sat with him in a carriage. 'Now what harm is there in saying "Lord Caesar", and in offering incense, and so on, and thus saving thyself?' But Polycarp, the aged Bishop of Smyrna, shook his head. Perhaps it was his legendary acquaintance with the apostle John in early days that steeled his courage. As Bishop of Smyrna, he would certainly have read the second of the seven letters in Revelation chapter 2. Were the words of that letter in his mind as he was led to the stadium?

'Do not be afraid of what you are about to suffer. I tell you, the devil will put some of you in prison to test you, and you will suffer persecution for ten days. Be faithful, even to the point of death, and I will give you the crown of life' (2:10).

In the stadium, the Roman Proconsul gave Polycarp every chance: 'Swear, and I will release thee; curse the Christ.' Polycarp's reply was memorable: *'Eighty and six years have I served him, and he hath done me no wrong; how then can I blaspheme my king who saved me?'*

Polycarp was burnt to death the same day. You can visit Izmir, his city, today and see the great Roman aqueducts that he would have known, still standing.

Polycarp's story is a vivid reminder that the letters of Christ to the seven churches were addressed to real situations and needs, to Christian people facing change, adversity and pressure – just as you and I do today. What do we find in these letters?

Each letter follows a familiar pattern. We find, first, a description of Christ, the author; then a word of approval or commendation for the church in question; next a message of correction – followed by a special command or encouragement; and, last of all, a promise to those who obey the message. Read through these brief letters, and observe this pattern for yourself.

We may not understand every one of the allusions in these messages, without the help of a good commentary. But join me on a lightning survey – because these letters are for *you!*

Ephesus – the backsliding church (2:1-7)
It was difficult to be a 'lampstand' for Jesus Christ in this great capital, with its theatre, libraries and superb seventy-

foot-wide main road, lined with columns, that led through the city to the impressive harbour. The heathen temple of Diana dominated everything!

Yet the Christians had done well there. No doubt the apostle Paul's two-year stay (Acts 19) had helped them to a true grasp of the apostolic truth. With flying colours they had passed the *service test* – 'your hard work' (v. 2); *the endurance test* – 'you have persevered and have endured hardships' (v. 3); and *the doctrine test* – 'you have tested those who claim to be apostles but are not' (v. 2). The Ephesian Christians saw through the teaching and practices of 'the Nicolaitans', a false group that threatened to infiltrate the Church. It was an impressive record.

There was only one flaw – but it was a vital one. *'You have forsaken your first love'* (v. 4). The flame that had burned so brightly at first was now flickering. The Christians in Ephesus were magnificent workers, and their orthodoxy was superb. But if a Church's love for Christ has cooled off, it will be reflected in everything; in its worship, its relationships and in its evangelistic impact. The stranger senses it on arrival. 'It is not virtue that can save the world or anyone in it, but love,' wrote Archbishop Temple. Love is the one indispensable element in Christ's people.

Smyrna – the suffering church (2:8-11)
The coach tour operators would have been proud to take you round the thriving commercial city of Smyrna. They would have led you, without fail, to the birthplace of Homer – to whom a public statue had been erected. From there you might have paid a visit to the Temple of Cybele. One thing you could be sure of – no guide party would ever have taken you to the local Christian church.

The Church at Smyrna – to be led one day by Polycarp – was *nothing*. It had no resources, no bank account. Persecution was on the way. Jewish opposition and slander was bitter. Poor Smyrna!

But to Christ ... *the Christians there were beautiful.* He saw them as perhaps the richest of all the seven churches. 'I know your afflictions and your poverty – yet you are rich!' (v. 9) Rich – the Greek New Testament at this point uses a term from which we get our word *plutocrats!*

Plutocrats ... and champions. If they could endure, the winner's crown of life would be theirs (v. 10). There was an arena at Smyrna – the allusion would not have been lost on Polycarp and his friends as they read the letter. There is no corrective word from Christ to this Church, no apparent defect. In Christianity, suffering and blessing go together. Smyrna was beautiful.

Pergamum – the compromising church (2:12-17)
You will have noticed by now that each letter begins with a description of the divine author, drawn from that initial vision that confronted John. Here Christ is 'him who has the sharp, double-edged sword' (v. 12). The Christians in Pergamum lived in a maze of 'religions', under the ultimate domination of the pervasive emperor-worship. Pergamum was Satan's residence! (v. 13).

The sharp sword of God's revealed truth in Christ was vitally necessary. There is always the danger of compromise in a situation of religious pluralism, and Christ can never be merely one of many viable alternatives. He stands alone. We must never forget Polycarp. We must not ignore Antipas (v. 13), evidently a martyr for Christ at Pergamum.

The Nicolaitans were here at this place too! It seems that they were the New Testament counterpart to Balaam, about whom we read in the Old Testament book of Numbers, chapters 22–24. Balaam was a gifted prophet, who should have known better than to compromise as he did with idolatry and immorality. He and the Nicolaitans shared in the same error – but the majority of believers at Pergamum stayed firm (v. 13).

Theirs would be the reward.

The reward of the hidden manna (v. 17) refers to the miraculously-supplied bread from heaven, about which we read in Exodus 16. Moses commanded that some of this be put inside a jar, at least initially, and stored inside the Ark of the Covenant (Exod. 16:33; Heb. 9:4). Centuries later, Jesus described *himself* as 'the living bread that came down from heaven' (John 6:51). He is the ultimate manna that satisfies.

And the white stone? This may refer to the stones of the Urim and Thummim, a form of casting lots, by which in earlier Old Testament times God gave his guidance (Exod. 28:30). The manna ... the white stone – they speak of God's provision and of God's further revelation. *In the end, this means more of Christ.* Could there be a greater reward for faithfulness?

Thyatira – the polluted church (2:18-29)
'I'm looking for the perfect church,' someone was reputed to have said to the celebrated Baptist preacher, C. H. Spurgeon.

'Well, when you find it,' replied Spurgeon, 'let me know. *But don't join it –* or you'll spoil it!'

Alas, all churches are imperfect, just as the church at Thyatira was. There was a problem woman there – tolerated as a member of the fellowship, but seen by the blazing, all-seeing eyes of Christ (v. 18) as a throw-back to the days of the notorious Baal-worshipping Jezebel of Old Testament times (1 Kings 21:25). She obviously had set herself up as a prophetess, and had gained some influence among the believers. False teaching and idolatrous immoral behaviour were causing havoc in the Church. Those who joined her would ultimately be overthrown with her.

But the 'overcomers' had a twofold promise coming to them. They would share in the messianic rule of Christ (verse 27 is a quotation from the messianic Psalm 2); and they would receive 'the morning star.' What is this star? We do not have to look outside the Bible for the right interpretations. The Bible interprets itself. Revelation 22:16 gives us the identification. It is Christ himself! And the place where this morning star will rise is in our hearts (2 Peter 1:19). Could there be a greater reward for faithfulness?

Sardis – the dying church (3:1-6)
The greatest days of the city of Sardis were over; and yet it was a city still reclining on its past. This spirit had crept into the Church too. The Christians there had the reputation of being alive and active, but – tragedy! Theirs was a name without life, a form without power, a facade without reality. The catchwords of their earlier better days were still remembered; they knew the right words and phrases ... but it was all a hollow sham. Sardis was a dead Church.

There is a way back from dead formalism – for a church or for an individual. It is the way taken by the Prodigal Son of our Lord's parable. *Remember ... repent* (v. 3). Can you remember those early days of enthusiasm for the things of God, for the Church, for prayer and the Bible? Let the memory trigger you into turning around in repentance. It means a U-turn.

There were just a few who had kept faithful in Sardis. Their reward was to walk in righteousness with Christ. In any 'dead' church, there is usually a tiny remnant who are holding on in prayer and faith for better days. Are you one such, as you read these words? God will reward you.

Philadelphia – the serving church (3:7-13)

I remember a letter plopping on to my door-mat many years ago. It was from a communist who resented having received a piece of Christian literature from our Church. It ended with the jibe, 'Your jammy little job will go for a Burton. And not before it is time.'

It certainly seemed that Christ's Church at Philadelphia (now the Turkish city of Alasehir) would hardly be missed by its critics if it was rubbed out. Its power was minimal (v. 8), it was hated by a Jewish element (v. 9) – and yet it was very precious to Christ. As in Smyrna's case, there is no word of divine criticism for Philadelphia. Three symbols come to our attention:

THE KEY (v. 7). What is this key of David? The answer lies in Isaiah 22:22, where it is written of the king's steward: 'I will place on his shoulder the key to the house of David; what he opens no-one can shut, and what he shuts no-one can open.' *Authority* is the emphasis here; the steward is taken as an illustration of Christ.

THE DOOR (v. 8). *Opportunity* is emphasized by this symbol. A Christian leader used to make this his regular prayer: 'Lord, give me eyes to see, and grace to seize, every opportunity for Thee.'

THE PILLAR (v. 12). *Permanence* is the emphasis. In a city shaken repeatedly by earthquakes, as Philadelphia was, this would have meant much. Permanence and stability would be the reward of faithful service given by the frail Church of Philadelphia.

Laodicea – the lukewarm Church (3:14-22)

Laodicea was a rich city – and insolent. When it was the victim of a terrible earthquake in AD 60, Tacitus, the Roman historian, tells us that it disdained to accept aid from the emperor Nero!

There is no word of divine commendation for the Church in Laodicea. Researchers tell us that near the city were hot springs. The water was piped to Laodicea, but by the time it arrived it was lukewarm – the reference was an apt one for a church that was neither hot nor cold (v. 16). 'Wretched, pitiful, poor, blind and naked' – is this the description of a Christian? Here was a church that had degenerated into nominal belief.

The way back is through repentance, and through receiving the Christ who knocks at the door of every life (vv. 19, 20).

* * *

'He who has an ear, let him hear what the Spirit says to the churches.'

These letters are for us too. They remind us that the work of Christ is done through very imperfect channels ... but they are the only channels he has chosen to use! Years ago, Trinity Episcopal School for Ministry in Pittsburg was opened. Alfred Stanway, its Australian principal, said at the opening: 'If other people knew you, like God knows you; all your faults and all your thoughts, all your sins, all the things in your heart that have been in there, all the wrong thoughts that you've ever had; *would they trust you with the kind of work that God trusts you with?* Here is the supreme confidence that God has in his own grace. He'll take the likes of you and me, and give you the privilege of being his servant. He's got to take people like you and me. He has no others.'

SUGGESTIONS FOR STUDY

Read on your own the first three chapters of Revelation. Study groups may wish to read together Revelation 1:9-20. The following questions may be discussed:

1. Look at verse 9 and the words 'suffering and kingdom'. What significance does the group see in this combination of words? Look up Acts 14:22. How far is this combination true of Christ himself, and of our own experience?

2. The seven churches. Let each group member 'adopt' a church for a few minutes, and try to see a parallel between it and some aspect of church life today. What is the Spirit saying to the Churches of our time?

3. Consider the vision of Christ in verses 12-16. Where is Christ; what does he look like, and what is he doing? Compare this scene with that described in Mark 9:2-7. In what way would this vision have actually helped John?

4. 'I am the First and the Last' (v. 17). What do these words tell us about Christ? Compare Isaiah 48:12 and Revelation 1:8; 22:13.

5. Think of your own fellowship or church for a moment. How is it accomplishing its calling as a lampstand (vv. 12, 20)? What is the secret – from this passage – of improving our effectiveness?

6. Look at verse 18. What would have been the effect of this truth on the first century? How does it affect your own thinking? Is it worth memorizing verses 17 and 18 in the Bible version of your preference?

7. What would you say is the keynote that comes out of the seven letters?

PART TWO

GOD IS ON THE THRONE

'Please don't be shocked if you hear that there is a revolution in Burundi, Uganda or Zaire. This is Africa! It's nothing when young countries get revolutions. They are going to get some more.

'But that does not mean that the Man of Galilee has vacated the throne! Christianity has never been scared of a revolution. Satan can roar like a lion, but he has no authority to shake the throne on which Jesus is sitting!'

Bishop Festo Kivengere of Uganda

4

THE ETERNAL THRONE

A fabulous display of fireworks burst over Sydney's Harbour Bridge, and the whole world saw it on television. December 31st 1999 had given way to January 1st 2000. As the fireworks died down, the single word *Eternity* was left emblazoned on the bridge in neon lighting, in letters ninety feet high. It shone out over the harbour waters for the rest of the night.

The display had been erected there in commemoration of one of Sydney's most celebrated citizens of the twentieth century. Back in the 1930s, Arthur Stace had been a homeless down-and-out. Going one day for a rock bun into St. Barnabas Church, Broadway, he was confronted with the message of salvation, and he became a Christian. As he put it later, 'I went in to get a rock bun, and came out with the Rock of Ages.'

The whole prospect of an Eternity with Christ riveted him, and he determined to face his fellow-citizens with the issue. From then on, night after night, he would chalk on Sydney's sidewalks, walls and any available surface, the word *Eternity*, in beautiful copperplate letters. Morning came, and commuters and shoppers would wonder at the word.

Arthur Stace kept this up for years. It is estimated that he may have chalked *Eternity* some million times in all. Eventually, a newspaper reporter determined to stay up all night and track down the mystery pavement artist – and the secret was out. Arthur became known as 'Mr. Eternity'. Sydney's remarkable tribute, that Millennium Eve, was to a man for whom eternity was a daily reality to live with and witness to.

Is it for you? The message of the Bible is that it can be – and should be. The book of Revelation has a great deal to portray in terms of the conflicts, persecutions and natural catastrophes that will face the believer of every age. But before we are ever allowed to come to this alarming catalogue, we are given a glimpse into the eternal dimension that governed Arthur Stace's outlook, the unseen rule and centre that lies behind everything that happens in this world ... the timeless throne of God.

This is basic to all of John's message. *Eternity.* These next two chapters (Rev. 4 and 5) are given, to prepare the reader for what lies ahead. We are taken behind the scenes of all that exists and happens. We come to the very centre of all power, and peer into eternity itself!

Step into chapter 4 of the Book of Revelation, and sense something of what John was allowed to experience in his amazing vision.

God's throne speaks to us of eternity
Every other throne can be shaken – but never that of God. His throne is permanent and secure. He lives for ever and ever (v. 10). The praise of the living creatures is ceaseless (v. 8).

This is the great reassurance of the prophecy. *God is in control.* True, we are not puppets on a string; we have been given free agency. We can rebel if we choose to do so, and create confusion and discord in God's world. Part of the angelic world is in rebellion, under the leadership of Satan, the fallen angel. We see something of his activity in the pages ahead of us – creating hatreds, deprivations and conflict. *Meanwhile*

God never leaves the throne. The centre of the whole outfit is permanently secure!

God's throne speaks to us of personality

'At once I was in the Spirit, and there before me was a throne in heaven with someone sitting on it' (4:2).

Someone ... What a relief!

We do not need to think of blindly-operating forces controlling our destiny. We do not take our guidance from the stars. We are not the victims of mere chance, fate or luck. There is personality at the centre of our universe. This makes the difference – to everything!

God's throne speaks to us of majesty

How reverently the apostle describes the view that met him! We should be careful not to read too much into the mention of 'jasper', 'carnelian', and 'emerald' (v. 3). It is enough to know that colours of brilliance shone from the different facets of the throne's divine occupant. A rainbow encircled the whole – surely a reminder of the firm covenant faithfulness of God pledged in Genesis 9:13. Everything here speaks of awe-inspiring majesty.

God's throne speaks to us of authority

A throne ... surrounded by other thrones (v. 4). Why twenty-four? This is a hint to us of the people of God across the centuries – the twelve tribes of the Old Testament and the twelve apostles of the New, combined together. These 'elders' seem to be angelic beings representing God's people on earth.

Behind all that we see happening in this world – the mistakes and sins of fallen, rebellious mankind – God is steadily working his purpose out. He has the ultimate rule. This is basic to the message of Revelation.

God's throne speaks to us of purity
The scene before John is shot through with goodness and holiness. The flashes of lightning and the rumbling of thunder (v. 5) are reminiscent of the giving of the Law to Moses at Mount Sinai (Exod. 19:16-23) – with its message of unapproachable holiness. The seven lamps speak of the Holy Spirit in the perfection of his attributes. The sea of glass speaks of shining transcendence, and the song of the living creatures around the throne is concerned again with God's holiness; here are representatives of Creation, and are like the beings described in Ezekiel 10:20, 21. Why four? Four seems to be a number for *nature* – the four corners of the earth ... the four winds (Rev. 7:1).

We find this concept of the Throne hard to believe, when bombarded by the pessimistic headlines of the world's press. Sometimes we feel dwarfed by the intimidating power structures of society. We cannot see what John was privileged to see; nevertheless the throne is there all right.

I remember once frying an egg.

'Dad,' said one of the family, 'you ought to put the lid on top of the frying pan.'

'I can't do that,' I replied, 'I have to *see* the egg.'

Naturally there are cooks more experienced in the ways of faith, who do not need to see the egg in the pan. Their faith, based upon the data of past events, tells them that all will be well!

For the Christian believer, there is no apparent sight of the throne of God. The sky seems closed off – *and yet it is not closed off for us*. By faith we know about God and his rule. The events of Christ's mission – his death, resurrection, ascension and gift of the Spirit – are enough. We have seen the unfolding story of the Church – and something inside says, 'There is a purpose being worked out. God is ruling. Christ is returning. Goodness will finally triumph. I am on the winning side.'

Let John's prophecy help your faith to soar as you read these inspired pages of the Revelation. It all starts here – with his vision of the throne that is for ever. But we have not covered every aspect of this vision yet. We must now deal with another factor in it – one which is absolutely vital.

For your reading
Revelation, chapter 4.

5

ENTER THE LAMB

Elisabeth and I were seated in London's Aldwych Theatre with our American host, Bronson Stocker – and I was confused. We had been taken to see Tom Stoppard's play *Hapgood,* and the plot wasn't making any sense to me. Not that we hadn't been warned in advance by our genial Texan mentor: 'Now Richard, you need to understand that the storyline is a little complicated. Keep alert in the opening moments particularly!'

I took the hint, and was on the edge of my seat as the curtain went up. In an instant there was action – plenty of it – fast and furious. My eyes were darting towards every corner of the stage, as I struggled to take in the rapid sequence of events. The added effect of strobe lighting did little to assist my thought-processes as the play progressed. My wife got the thread, but to this day I couldn't tell you what *Hapgood* was really about. I like my stories simple!

'*Wonderful, Bronson. Thanks ever so much for a terrific evening.*' We were out in the night air of London, heading for the Strand. We passed the theatre billboard. On it, words from a newspaper review had been highlighted: 'You don't have to be Einstein to understand this play ... *but it helps*'.

Read the opening sentences of Revelation 5, and you can detect a parallel frustration in the universal attempt to crack the meaning of life. In John's vision, the divine occupant of the eternal throne is holding a sealed scroll, but no one seems capable of opening or understanding it:

> 'But no-one in heaven or on earth or under the earth could open the scroll or even look inside it. I wept and wept because no-one was found who was worthy to open the scroll or look inside' (5:3, 4).

What is this scroll, with writing on both sides, and sealed with seven seals? The following chapters in the book of Revelation indicate that it is the scroll containing the secrets of our world's affairs and its history. The cry goes up for one who is worthy to open the scroll, interpret its meaning and actually carry it through – someone who can make real sense of our existence and our destiny. *Who can unravel the plot?*

What about some of the wisest men we have ever produced? Plato? Socrates? Isaac Newton? George Washington? Albert Einstein?

No. No man, no angel even, has the necessary qualifications to interpret history ... to open the scroll. It's a question of worthiness, and no one – it seems – is found worthy. John, in his vision, begins to weep.

Of course, it is a terrible thing to be unable to solve the mystery of life. Many have made the attempt. Many others sink into apathy, with the futility of it all. At various times in history the despair of thinking people has reached a kind of crisis. This happened in the first century AD, with the mounting phobia of **death.** It was no coincidence that, simultaneously, the resurrection of Christ began to be heralded by the Church, gossiped on the highways of the Roman Empire, scrawled upon the walls of the catacombs. There was an answer!

It happened again in the Middle Ages, as the fear of **guilt** gripped the minds of philosophers, artists and preachers. What happened? The message of the Cross was rediscovered in Europe, banishing guilt and leading millions to the assurance of sins forgiven and acceptance before God.

Is the process being repeated in our own day? Undeniably it is – and the phobia in thinking circles today is concerned with meaninglessness. We see this in contemporary writing, in art, and in some of those strange plays that appear to have no plot. *There is no plot* – that is the message! No meaning in life, no objective truth about our world and its destiny – there is nothing there.

What is our Christian answer? It comes with clarifying, overwhelming force in terms of the books of Genesis and Revelation! The beginning and the end, creation and the consummation of all things. The mighty truth of God at work in man's creation, in the shape and goal of his story, tells us all we need to know. The shackles of rigid determinism melt away before its onslaught. The negative gospel of a meaningless universe shatters into pieces.

Do not weep, comes the message of chapter five:

'" See, the Lion of the tribe of Judah, the Root of David, has triumphed. He is able to open the scroll and its seven seals." Then I saw a Lamb, looking as if it had been slain, standing in the centre of the throne ...' (5:5, 6).

In all of our human story, and throughout the courts of heaven, precisely one figure emerges with sufficient qualifications to unravel the mystery, and to open the scroll – and to claim the title deeds of the world!

Christ is the explanation of this world's affairs

I was once leading a mission at one of our English universities. Over coffee a student came up to me after I had been speaking.

'I've been thinking about these things, and I've become a Christian tonight,' he told me.

I was glad for him and encouraged him. But then he went on, 'There's only one thing that bothers me at the back of my mind.'

'What's that?' I asked.

'I just hope that I won't find that Jesus Christ, whom I now believe in, doesn't prove to be only a part of something bigger than himself – some bigger system, like Hinduism, for example. What does Christianity say on this point?'

I readily showed him a New Testament passage that exactly met his query:

> 'He is the image of the invisible God, the firstborn over all creation. For by him all things were created: things in heaven and on earth, visible and invisible, whether thrones or powers or rulers or authorities; all things were created by him and for him. He is before all things, and in him all things hold together' (Col. 1:15-17).

'This refers to Jesus?' persisted the student.

I hastened to assure him that it did.

'Then my search is over!' exulted my new Christian friend. He looked ready to leap out of his skin with happiness.

It is a common feeling shared by millions, who recognize in Jesus Christ the hereditary Lord of all creation, the one who is both God and Man. Only he can qualify to solve the riddle of our existence. So John learns in his vision. 'See, the Lion of the tribe of Judah, the Root of David, has triumphed.

He is able to open the scroll and its seven seals.' The next sentence is illuminating, however.

Christ is the fulfilment of this world's affairs
For as we read on, there is a surprise. John was looking for a Lion – a picture of strength and triumph. What did he see? 'Then I saw a Lamb, looking as if it had been slain' (5:6).

Leon Morris, in his excellent Tyndale commentary on Revelation, makes the observation that most nations, looking for a symbol of strength, choose powerful animals or birds of prey – the Russian bear, the British lion, the American spread eagle and so on. 'It is only the Kingdom of Heaven that would dare to use as its symbol of might, not the Lion for which John was looking but the helpless Lamb, and at that, a slain Lamb.'

Or, to be more accurate, a Lamb with the *appearance* of having been slain, for it is now all too obviously alive, as it takes the tantalizing scroll (v. 7). Has the message registered? It is as the *once-crucified* Son of God that the Lamb emerges as uniquely qualified to unlock the eternal secrets and give true significance to our existence. The Cross is at the centre. Only through the crucified Christ can we establish a relationship with God, and thus with the source of life in our universe. He alone could fulfil God's saving purposes for the world.

Christ is the completion of this world's affairs
The Lamb is depicted as having seven horns – symbolizing perfect power. He has seven eyes – interpreted here as the seven spirits of God; a symbol seemingly of perfect spiritual vitality, coupled with perfect all-seeing omniscience.

It is the ascended Jesus that we are presented with; once-crucified, but now with his work done and completed. Consequently the praise breaks out around the throne, from the living creatures, the elders, and innumerable angels. Meditate unhurriedly upon these words of praise (vv. 9-14), and make them your own!

How John's readers must have found encouragement in these great fourth and fifth chapters of the Apocalypse! They were hemmed in by imperial and religious pressures on every side. They were challenging the society of their day with their claim that Jesus was Lord – the only Lord. In this they faced the inevitable hostility of Rome's emperor, as well as that of alien ideologies. Theirs was a day of religious pluralism – but pluralism is out for the individual who has caught a glimpse of the Lamb with the scroll! Who can compare with the one who opens the seals and makes sense of existence?

> Come and see the shining hope
>   that Christ's apostle saw;
> on the earth, confusion,
>   but in heaven an open door,
> where the living creatures
>   praise the Lamb for evermore:
> Love has the victory for ever!

> Amen, he comes! to bring his own reward!
> Amen, praise God! for justice now restored;
> kingdoms of the world become
>   the kingdoms of the Lord:
> Love has the victory for ever!

From Revelation 4–5
© Christopher Idle

This hymn, with two further verses, is set to *Marching through Georgia* (Jubilate Hymns).

For your reading
Revelation, chapter 5.

6

RIDING THROUGH HISTORY

I have always enjoyed watching indoor tennis, as played by the legendary greats, from McEnroe and Borg, to Cash and Agassi. But until a certain November night, I had never had the inside view of a match, being – like every other spectator – up in the stands.

One night it was different. I had indeed seen the big match from the stands, and when it was over I made for the exit – and for a cup of coffee. But I was intercepted.

'Like to come through into the dressing room?'

It was a cheerful BBC tennis correspondent who stopped me. We had become friends earlier, through a common involvement in the game – and also in Christian fellowship.

I followed the BBC man into a room away from the lights and the crowd. Lying on a couch, surrounded by masseurs and other assistants, was the same American I had seen battling it out minutes earlier on court. I had known him for some years, as a fine Christian. It was then that I got an altogether different view of what had been happening – *and a fascinatingly different interpretation.*

It is another kind of court that we are dealing with as we come *behind the scenes*, here in the book of Revelation, and into the main body of the prophecy at chapters 6 and 7. The seven seals that are about to be opened will give us a panoramic view of history – from the inside view of the Church of

Christ. It is not history exactly, but *interpreted* history that we are introduced to here. You will not find any reference to the Hundred Years War, the discovery of America, or the Boxer Uprising! If you look for such incidents, you have missed the point completely.

In this, our 'parallelist' interpretation, we believe ourselves to be looking at the total age spanned by Christ's first and second comings. It is the age which included the Roman Empire of John's day, but it also includes our own generation. What are we going to understand of history from the Church's point of view, as we read in chapters 6 and 7 of the four horsemen, of the slain martyrs, of the sky receding like a scroll, and of the 144,000?

The Church should expect to live adventurously
It is the *Church* that is particularly concerned to know the contents of the scroll, as we were reminded in chapter 5. Furthermore, it is the Church's divine leader who alone is qualified to break the seals and reveal the contents of the scroll. If it is Christ who oversees the unfolding events of history, then his people may take heart, however forbidding the events that take place. It must have been with trust and confidence that John, in his vision, saw the first of the seals broken:

> 'I looked, and there before me was a white horse! Its rider held a bow, and he was given a crown, and he rode out as a conqueror bent on conquest' (6:2).

Who is this first of four horsemen? I used to think that this represented Christ – in his beneficial conquest of love across the world. Then my view was challenged by several Bible commentators who questioned whether Christ could merely take an apparently equal place among three other horsemen

(vv. 3-8), all of ominous identity. Was not this rider on a white horse representative of all the aggressive attempts at conquest that have persisted in history? I wavered.

But now I have come back again in my thinking! Always, in the Revelation, *white* seems to depict purity (e.g., 1:14; 2:17; 7:14; 20:11). Then the rider is wearing a *crown,* and we observe elsewhere that Christ is so crowned (14:14). None of the other riders are. Further, with very few exceptions *conquest* is seen in the Revelation as the work of Christ (e.g., 3:21; 5:5; compare also John 16:33).

But Revelation 19:11 seems to be conclusive. There we read of a white horse, with Christ as its obvious rider who, with justice 'judges and makes war'. The identity of the first rider seems unmistakable in chapter 6. What does this point to?

Under the leadership of Christ, in his victorious mission, the Church must take heart! The Lamb has triumphed over death and darkness. He is the true interpreter of all the ages. He is ascended, and is crowned. As we go out to serve and communicate in *his* Name we should expect victory. He is the rider on the white horse. He is the Conqueror!

But of course, there is another side to this. Too many Christian people embrace an unrealistic, romantic view of the advance of the kingdom of God. They seem to imagine that there will be no casualties in the battles ahead. Frequently, when adversity and testing comes, their naïve triumphalistic beliefs collapse like a pack of cards.

The Church should expect to live dangerously
On to the next seals. Three more horsemen follow, one after another. It is not difficult to see what they stand for. Throughout our church age we have known what slaughter on a grand scale is all about, as represented by the rider on the red horse (6:3, 4). The rider is said 'to take peace from

the earth and to make men slay each other'. These conflicts are with us today.

The black horse? Famine is clearly indicated (vv. 5, 6). When I was about seven, I was in a famine. Our family lived in Africa, and I recall the year when the rains failed. Everyone went hungry; some people died. Never before, and never since, have I eaten such extraordinary meals. But these hard times are a frequent occurrence in many parts of the world when, as we observe from verse 6, the luxuries of the worldly rich are untouched.

Then the pale horse of death (vv. 7, 8). Here is death, by a variety of means. The indication is that one in four are likely to die violently or unnaturally. The Christian community is not to be surprised by this phenomenon; we have already been warned.

When the fifth seal is opened, martyrdom stares us in the face (vv. 9-11). I remember meeting a martyr. His name was Janani Luwum. He was an Anglican archbishop in Uganda at the time of the hideous regime led by president Idi Amin. For his courageous stand against violence he himself was shot. His body was taken by the military regime far north for a secret burial, away from the publicity. But the Christians of that area knew. Before the burial, they quietly went by night to inspect the coffin, and established that it indeed contained the body of their archbishop. Then, when the burial was over, the church members maintained a round-the-clock vigil, twenty four hours a day, by the graveside for the next few weeks. A Christian martyr deserves the highest respect of all. There have been millions such. One day it may be you. . .

The sixth seal is quite evidently of a futuristic nature! (vv. 12-17). What is John describing? It is no less than the cosmic disturbance that will be associated with the final break-up of the world as we know it. You will find similar language in Isaiah 34:4. Various interests will be adversely affected (v. 15): *imperial interests* (kings and princes); *martial interests* (the generals); *financial interests* (the rich); *influential interests* (the mighty) and *communal interests* (slave and free man).

The wrath of the Lamb will be in evidence, and who can stand up in the day of judgement that ends our history? For we shall all be there.

There is one more seal to be opened, but first ... an interlude! It contains a reassurance for the believer.

The Church should expect to live fearlessly
'Are you in the 144,000?' I once asked Jehovah's Witnesses, who had come to our door.

'No, no,' I was told. 'We know that we can't be.'

'But I am!' I replied. My statement surprised them.

Here, in chapter 7, is a stylized number, signifying the company of God's people across the centuries. It is not an elitist group, selected out of the body of believers, as the Jehovah's Witnesses have surmised. For we read of the 144,000 elsewhere that they 'had been redeemed from the earth' (14:3).

This is not a literal number. It is rather *a diagram of the Church*, with its multiple of the figure twelve. So suggests Michael Wilcock in his commentary (*I Saw Heaven Opened*, Inter-Varsity Press).

Let's be careful about numbers in the Apocalypse. The Revelation is intended to *inspire*, not to bemuse! There are these different numbers, and they are to be taken as symbols. *Twelve* seems to be the number for the Church (twelve tribes of Israel, twelve apostles). *Four* appears to be the number for nature (e.g. Rev. 7:1), and *ten* seems to symbolize a rounded-off completeness in a given situation. And *seven*? This comes up everywhere! The seven churches, the seven seals ... and there are plenty more instances to follow! Many call it the perfect number. It is certainly a *basic* number – think of the seven days of creation, or the seven days of the week. Wilcock declares: 'As the classical dramatists of England habitually wrote in five-beat blank verse, and those of France in six-beat rhyming couplets, so these seven-beat rhythms seem to be the natural cadences of the voice of God.'

So let us return to the 144,000. Chapter 7 is one of the most inspiring and moving in the Bible. It depicts the Church, the people of God, battered and threatened, often persecuted, but nevertheless fearless, as:

The Church Militant. We are out in the arena, exposed and vulnerable – and yet sealed by God (v. 3). Elsewhere, too, believers in Jesus Christ are declared to be *sealed* (Eph. 1:13; 4:30). What does this mean?

  – It is the stamp of ownership.
  – It is the mark of genuineness.
  – It is the guarantee of security.

God's presence, by the Holy Spirit, is what marks out the true disciple from the merely nominal Christian. How can you tell if you are sealed?

There are a number of telltale signs! Are you someone who has a trust in Jesus Christ, and a love for him? Do you find yourself more and more wanting to meet with others who are in his Church? Does the truth of God exert an increasing, magnetic pull upon you? Do you find yourself in distress when you fall into the old, wrong habits? Is it *difficult,* living as a Christian and fighting against evil? If the answer is 'Yes', it's a good sign! You are in the Church Militant!

The Church Triumphant. The Church Triumphant describes those for whom the fight is over – they are with God (vv. 9-17). The term 144,000 is not used here – it is simply 'a great multitude'. These are the people who have come through the great trials of which we have been reading. They learnt what forgiveness meant in their earthly pilgrimage (v. 14); they followed the Lamb and served him during their lives – now they serve him at the throne (v. 15). Notice the amazing development – the *Lamb* has become the *Shepherd* (v. 17)!

So we have taken a ride through history. We have seen something of what the Church of God can expect in this era between the two comings of Jesus Christ. These signs and patterns are not to be taken like a count-down towards the End. We cannot construct from them a time-table of world events and chronology. To quote Stephen Travis: 'They are not like the signs which say "End of Motorway 1 mile". They are more like the hazard lights which warn us of dangers along the way' (*The Jesus Hope*, IVP).

The chapter ends, and we are introduced to another set of seven – the Trumpets!

What's that you say? Something left out?

Ah – the seventh seal!

It seems, in fact, that the seventh seal IS the Seven Trumpets.

SUGGESTIONS FOR STUDY

Read on your own chapters 4–6 of the Revelation. Study groups may wish to read together chapter 5. The following questions may help the discussion:

1. Are there any in the group who ever felt as John felt, when trying to understand the meaning of life? (Rev. 5:4). Can you put your experience into words?

2. Try and enumerate some of the factors that uniquely qualify Jesus Christ as the true interpreter of history (v. 5). How do some of the world's great thinkers compare with him?

3. In what way does verse 7 seem reminiscent of an event in Christ's early life in Nazareth? Compare your findings with Luke 4:14-22. What aspects of Christ's person does this action of his highlight?

4. What do you learn about God's rule from this chapter, in view of the evils described in the following chapter.

5. Invite members of the group to say something of what they appreciate from one of the three songs of angelic praise (vv. 9-14).

6. How does the concept of God's throne help our own prayers?

PART THREE

THE TRUMPETS ARE SOUNDING

'God whispers to us in our pleasures, speaks to us in our consciences, but shouts to us in our pains; it is his megaphone to rouse a deaf world.'

C. L. Lewis, *The Problem of Pain*
(Collins, 1940, quoted by permission)

7

THE UNHEEDING WORLD

Shortly after noon on 10th April 1912, my mother – then aged nine – watched fascinated as the *Titanic*, on its maiden voyage, slid majestically through the Solent, outside Southampton. Little did she realize that she was witnessing the beginning of one of the most talked-about sea disasters of all time. Four days later the great liner had plunged to its icy fate at the bottom of the Atlantic.

So often it takes a crisis to expose the empty values of unbelieving materialism. The *Titanic* abounds in illustrations. One passenger left his cabin for the last time, leaving behind some 300,000 dollars in bonds and preferred stock. Instead he took with him three oranges. A Scotsman clinging to a spar in the bitter Atlantic night listened to the words of Christian counsel from a Glasgow preacher, John Harper. The preacher himself finally sank beneath the waves but, as the Scotsman put it later, 'There, alone in the night and with two miles of water under me, I believed. I am John Harper's last convert.'

It takes less than a *Titanic* – or a war – however, to rock complacency and upturn human scales of value. It only takes a coronary, or a bereavement or unemployment – and suddenly we are looking for answers about life and its meaning, answers about this world ... and the next ... and God.

All this relates to the theme of the Seven Trumpets that is unfolded for us from Revelation, chapter 8. As we studied the seven seals in chapters 6 and 7, we were seeing something of world events as affecting the Church. Now we retrace, and go over the whole ground again, seeing that same period between Christ's two comings – *but this time from the point of view of the unbelieving world.* There is a significant pause as we come to the trumpets, ushered in by the last of the seven seals:

'When he opened the seventh seal, there was silence in heaven for about half an hour' (8:1).

What is this interlude that precedes the trumpets? It includes a silence – perhaps to heighten the immensity of what is about to follow; the silence before the storm! For these are *warning trumpets* that are about to feature in the vision. We find a similar idea expressed in Ezekiel 33:3. There are other ingredients in this interlude. The prayers of God's people (vv. 3, 4) evidently play a real part in the working out of God's plan – and these are linked with the action of God (the fire of verse 5). Men and women pray; God acts.

Part of his action is in the form of warning trumpets of judgement. Let us think about this for a moment.

Some years ago I was driving from the Swedish mainland to the islands of Tjörn and Orust off the west coast. To get there you have to pass over the famous and very beautiful Tjörn Bridge. On this occasion, however, I was unable to use the bridge. It was down. A tanker, some weeks earlier, had run into one of the bridge supports, and had brought the whole immense structure down into the water.

On that dreadful night car after car had plunged over the broken bridge, headlights blazing, into the sea below – to the terrible distress of those still on the tanker, who could do nothing to warn the drivers.

It is later that the thought breaks surface: *it could have been me*. Occurrences like this make us all stop for a moment and reflect. They come as a warning that we should never take life for granted. It is not that such events are a direct judgement upon the particular victims involved. Jesus once spoke of an accident in Siloam, when eighteen people were killed by a falling tower:

'Do you think they were more guilty than all the others living in Jerusalem? I tell you, no! But unless you repent, you too will all perish' (Luke 13:4, 5).

It will be my turn all too soon! That ought to be our reaction; it is one of humility and repentance. C. S. Lewis' famous remark (see page 65) can be applied to the warning trumpets of Revelation 8–10.

As we take in the vision of the seven trumpets, we can see how they fit in with our Christian world-view. *Built into* the way in which we look at our existence is the idea of imperfection, fallenness and judgement. This world can never provide us with a Utopian ideal; those who look for it or expect it will consistently be disappointed. *We do not think like that.* All along the road we are to expect adversity – and storms:

A storm on land (8:6, 7)
It is indeed a wonderful world to live in – but it is not without its hazards. At any moment devastation can hit some part of the earth. Not *all* the earth, we observe – for these are not final judgements. This seems to be the idea behind the *third* that is repeated in these opening trumpets of warning. Take nothing for granted; the earth is a desirable home for mankind, but a vulnerable home!

A storm at sea (8:8, 9)

'A third of the sea turned into blood ... ' This is reminiscent of the plagues of Egypt by which Pharaoh of old was warned (Exod. 7:14-21). But perhaps the vision also reminded some of John's readers of Pompeii and Vesuvius! In every generation we can identify similar natural disasters. In these sentences, it is the sea, and the life of the sea that is partially affected.

A storm of pollution (8:10, 11)

Here, in the rivers and springs, are symbolized the natural resources for the sustaining of human life. Yes, this *is* reminiscent of Egypt's plagues at the time of Moses. Think of how the Nile itself, symbol of the strength and life of Egypt, was threatened at the command of God (Exod. 7:24). Every time a drought takes place or a tidal wave causes widespread pollution, human beings in their frailty are once again reminded of their utter dependence upon God, and of the fact that they stand under judgement.

A cosmic storm (8:12)

Is this, perhaps a piece of futuristic writing? It certainly accords with Christ's pronouncement that: 'There will be signs in the sun, moon and stars ... for the heavenly bodies will be shaken' (Luke 21:25, 26). When darkness swept over Egypt in Pharaoh's day (Exod. 10:21, 22), it must have come as an eerie hint that one day the world was going to end!

But there is more to come, in John's vision of the trumpets, as further warnings are given (8:13).

An occult storm (9:1-11)

Have you ever seen a locust swarm? I have. A big one is an amazing sight, as the whole sky is blotted out by millions of the voracious insects. If you are driving a car, you have to stop. Once the swarm settles, everything green disappears in one night.

But the locusts of chapter 9 hurt not the crops, but people! The reason for this appears in verses 2 and 3. They come from below. The message seems to be that if we will not respond to the saving acts of God in Christ – and are not sealed by him (v. 4) – then it is always possible that we may open ourselves to the alien power of strange, destructive forces that are satanic in origin. It is part of God's judgement, with the accompanying message, *Repent!*

A military storm (9:13-19)

War is contrary to the loving purposes of God; it stems from the rebellion that has taken hold of our race. Nevertheless, it can be used in God's design as a warning for unbelievers, reminding them of their insecurity outside of Christ. How many thousands have turned to God in time of war!

But why is war seen in verse 14 to come from the Euphrates? Perhaps because it represents Assyria and Babylon – symbolic down the ages of fighting fury and hostility. War is a terrible thing ... and yet! 'Everyone has noticed,' says C. S. Lewis, 'how hard it is to turn our thoughts to God when everything is going well with us.'

Six trumpets and now – as with the seals – there is a delay between the sixth and seventh trumpets. As we move on to chapter 10 we notice, with the close of chapter 9, how rare a phenomenon true repentance is, no matter how many warnings! The 'God-get-me-out-of-this-trench-and-I'll-believe-in-you' form of prayer can be forgotten very quickly once the threats are lifted.

The interlude of chapter 10 seems to be there to heighten the importance of the seventh trumpet. It takes the form of *an assurance* (vv. 1-3), *a prohibition,* (v. 4), *a vindication* (vv. 5-7) and a *commissioning* (vv. 8-11). It is a personal revelation to John himself. A massive angelic figure – clearly with a message and an authority of universal significance – appears to John, the great voice being answered by the revelation of the seven thunders. We will never know what the seven thunders portended! Their secret was meant only for the apostle. Just as Albert Einstein took with him to the grave certain scientific secrets considered too dangerous to be released, so only John was to be entrusted with the secrets of the seven thunders. Here is a firm discouragement of those would-be 'prophets' who imagine that they have the full run-down of world events at their fingertips. They have not! There is a whole area of knowledge that is kept from us.

All that *is* revealed for us to know, however, will come to pass, as predicted. So comes the promise of the angel, in verses 5-7. John will be vindicated in his prophecy – it is all going to happen!

Are you waiting for the seventh trumpet? We must wait a little longer still. John receives a commission in the form of a scroll (vv. 8-11). This ministry that he is to fulfil will have its combination of sweetness and bitterness. Any person reading this page, who is already projected into some form of Christian ministry, will be familiar with the experience. To have some small part in serving the interests of God upon this world – to be his mouthpiece – is the most satisfying and fulfilling of all privileges. But it tears you apart as well! You work and you speak in the cause of truth, but not everybody is listening. The trumpets sound out their warning – and to you may fall the demanding task of being a trumpet. But it's the old story of the *Titanic* again; of the Tjörn Bridge ... of an unheeding world.

For your reading
Revelation, chapters 8–10.

8

THE UNDYING CHURCH

'Please, can we talk with you?'

They were two soldiers, armed to the teeth with machine guns. It was the end of an open-air concert in the heart of Africa. The music of Garth Hewitt had drawn thousands along to some thirty such events in the course of a hectic twelve-day tour on behalf of the national Church. Garth had done the singing, I the preaching. We had just finished concert number twenty-seven!

We turned to the soldiers. 'Yes, how can we help?'

'We want to follow Jesus,' came the reply.

It was a moving experience to talk, and then to pray with the two men under the trees, in the middle of one of Africa's scarred, pot-holed cities. How we loved the country and its beautiful people!

In a land, which had staggered from crisis to crisis, it seemed to be the Church that consistently had the greatest power with the people. At times it had known severe oppression, but the power remained undiminished. Now we were seeing it at work again in the lives of our soldier friends.

Come to Revelation chapter 11, and we can recognize the pattern there. Yes, I know that you're waiting for that seventh trumpet – can you wait a little longer? For we must look at the *two witnesses* next. Who are they? They are the Church, God's people across the ages. They are the Christians of East

Timor. They are the Christians of the Sudan. They are the Christians of imperial Rome. They are you and me. Once again we resume our scanning of the whole picture! What do we see?

The squeezing of the Church (11:1, 2)
In his vision, John is told to go and measure the temple of God; that is, to sanctify it – but to distinguish between its sanctuary and the outer courts. The language is borrowed from Ezekiel 42:20. Those in the sanctuary are numbered. They are the insiders, and they are safe. They are God's own people. But the outer courts are vulnerable – they are for the peripheral, the careless, the nominal believers. Oppression sets in, as the holy city is trampled for forty-two months.

The real Church is safe. This does not mean that there are not casualties and martyrdoms; there are. But the Church remains intact throughout this period of adversity. It is what we are to expect throughout our Christian era. We were promised no less from our founder:

> 'In this world you will have trouble. But take heart! I have overcome the world' (John 16:33).

But simultaneously, another pattern of Christian history emerges in our passage.

The spreading of the Church (11:3-6)
Enter the two witnesses, the shutting up of the sky, the plagues on the earth and the 1,260 days! What does it all mean? *Think about it.* Read the passage again, remembering all the time that the Bible interprets itself; we don't have to indulge in fancy guesswork to arrive at the meaning of a passage. If

you have read the Bible before, even if only a little, it is possible that the ideas confronting you here will remind you of incidents and persons that you have encountered elsewhere in Scripture. Think carefully now...

How did you get on? Clue number one must lie in verse 6:

'These men have power to shut up the sky so that it will not rain during the time they are prophesying; and they have power to turn the waters into blood and to strike the earth with every kind of plague as often as they want.'

Have you got it? Yes, they are Elijah and Moses! Elijah, the most powerful of all the Old Testament prophets, had – at God's command – pronounced a period of drought upon the land (1 Kings 17:1). And Moses ... well, most of us are acquainted with the plagues of Egypt; with that other extraordinary period of ascendancy for the people of God. And, of course, Moses had been the great lawgiver ...

The Law and the Prophets ... Moses and Elijah. They are the two witnesses, symbolizing the powerful mission and outreach of the Church. Here is a picture of *authority*, reinforced by mention of the two olive trees and the two lampstands (a clear reference to two missionary representatives in Zechariah 4:11-14).

The two witnesses together symbolize a period of great ascendancy and power for God's people, lasting for ... how long? 1,260 days. Why ... that's forty-two months – the same period in which the Church faces the wilderness of opposition and squeezing. Think again, and you realize that forty-two months is equivalent to three and a half years exactly. Does that ring any bells for enthusiastic Bible readers? Of course it does!

'Elijah was a man just like us. He prayed earnestly that it would not rain, and it did not rain on the land for three and a half years' (James 5:17).

It all comes together. Elijah's period out in the wilderness was one of great opposition to the people of God, but it was also a time of immense influence – during which the prophet even had power to shut up the sky. It lasted for exactly three and a half years. This is taken in the Revelation as a symbol of our present Christian era. When we pray, we may expect results. When we proclaim the Good News in the power and energy of the Holy Spirit, we may look for things to happen. We are in the testing, but powerful period of the Two Witnesses! Ever since Christ's first coming, we have seen the spreading of the Church. Adversity and Christian growth walk together.

The silencing of the Church (11:7-10)
Is this futuristic? Yes and no. No, because we have frequently seen the phenomenon of the Church's apparent demise, only for a miracle to take place. Two centuries ago, Voltaire predicted that within a century the Bible would be an obsolete book and would have gone out of circulation. He was not to know that a century later his own Parisian residence would have been converted into a missionary centre, a Bible depot!

But there is also a definite futurist element here, in the rise and victory of 'the beast'. More about this being later. The indication is that when the time of Christian witness has been completed, there will be a short period (only three and a half days, as compared with the three and a half years of verse 3). The Church's voice will appear to have been silenced. Wickedness (Sodom and Egypt, v. 8) will appear to have gained the victory. No longer will people's consciences be troubled by the two witnesses (v. 10). The celebrations will begin. The Church is dead! But then comes the turning of the tables.

The rising of the Church (11:11-13)
The defeat of the Church is short-lived. It is heaven that has the last word, as God acts on behalf of his own in victorious and vindicating power. Evil is thwarted. Goodness has triumphed! So certain is the outcome, that John writes his prophecy in the past tense. It is as good as over.

The triumph of the Church is accompanied by the disarray of its enemies. At the end of time, events will cause even the bitterest of Christ's foes to acknowledge – albeit grudgingly – his power and victory (vv. 12, 13).

It is said that the cat has nine lives. The Church has infinitely more. Squeezed and hemmed in down the ages, it nevertheless exercises a power and an influence in the lives of millions. Threatened with extinction at various times, it continues to rise again. We say this in no triumphalistic spirit. The Christian world weeps when its members in any one place come under the jackboot or the firing squad. For these are God's precious people. They are the Christians of East Timor. They are the Christians of the Sudan. They are the Christians of imperial Rome. They are you and me.

You are wondering about the seventh trumpet. May we keep that for the next chapter?

For your reading
Revelation 11:1-14.

9

THE UNENDING REIGN

Regent Street in London provides a fascinating cake-mix of the world's nations. The next time you are visiting our capital, take an unhurried walk from Piccadilly Circus along this vast bazaar, containing some of the world's most famous stores. When you get to Oxford Circus, pause for a moment as you look north, along Upper Regent Street.

That is, if you can! The crowds will be swirling around you. Faces, hairstyles, languages and clothes merge together in amazing kaleidoscopic variations – an international parade – and you are part of it!

Then, as you look ahead, you see the outlines of the grey stone building that has served as the headquarters of the BBC since 1931. Just next to it is silhouetted the distinctive spire of the church of All Souls, Langham Place.

I like to think of that spire acting as a silent witness – as the cars, London taxis and red double-decker buses wind their restless way round the top end of Regent Street, past All Souls and the BBC, and into Portland Place – home of the embassies. The spire points heavenwards, as if to say, 'There could be another dimension to the lives of you tourists and entrepreneurs, you communicators and politicians. Raise your eyes above the power structures and exhaust fumes of your city! Look forward to a better and permanent kingdom!' This relates to the long-awaited seventh trumpet:

'The seventh angel sounded his trumpet, and there were loud voices in heaven, which said: "The kingdom of the world has become the kingdom of our Lord and of his Christ, and he will reign for ever and ever" ' (Rev. 11:15).

'The kingdom of the world … the kingdom of our Lord' – there is the contrast, and it is an immense one. Below, there is discord and confusion; above, we shall know harmony and order. In this way the seven trumpets conclude with the angelic acclamation of the reign of Christ. True, he is Lord already; but we have yet to see the final act. The Master of the World has yet to take over conclusively from the dictators, the business consortiums, the generals and the power manipulators.

The world has yet to see fair and just rule consistently exercised. The tissue of civilization is even now only paper-thin. Great empires have come and gone, frequently leaving a trail of human desolation. The world has seen the Babylonians take the centre of the stage, followed by the Medo-Persians, Greek and Roman empires. How much lasting good did they achieve for the world?

Last century we saw Hitler's bid for supremacy. How short a time did it take him to plunge the world into conflict and ruin his own country! Millions of individuals were involved in the devastation. Later we saw the high hopes of black Africa dashed in country after country, because few leaders seemed able to stand against the demoralizing corruption that power brings.

In the west, politicians lurch from one policy to another in a world that is reeling under a crisis of authority and government. Marxism had its chance, but left only a legacy of empty promises and crushed liberties.

Over against all the mismanagement of our world, generation by generation, a single trumpet note of hope soars upwards like the spire of All Souls. George Frederick Handel amplified the message in his inspired *Messiah*. 'And he shall reign for ever and ever.' The twenty-four elders take up the theme in their song of worship and praise (11:16-18).

We have already seen several of these outbursts of praise in the Apocalypse. We shall see more! But what is praise? It is more than a mere exclamation of joy. If we think that by singing 'Hallelujah!' we have been praising, we must think again. It is not praise for me to say to my wife, 'Elisabeth, I praise you. Oh I praise you ... yes, indeed, I praise you.' If I can only say that, I deserve all I get! Let me rather say, 'Liz, that was a wonderful pizza. I don't really know anyone who can make pizzas as you do.' Now that *is* praise!

Look carefully at the great passages of praise in the Bible. What are the men and angels doing in these instances? They are not simply babbling *Hallelujah*, or *Praise God!* and leaving it at that. *They are making great affirmations about God and his mighty works.* Never devalue the currency of praise. Do it the way Handel did, and go for praise that is truly biblical.

> 'We give thanks to you, Lord God Almighty, who is and who was, because you have taken your great power and have begun to reign' (v. 17).

And what will God's reign be like in its full and final form?

It will be all-embracing and universal, for it will take over from all human authority. 'The government will be on his shoulders,' exulted the prophet of old (Isa. 9:6).

It will be everlasting and permanent, for he will reign for ever and ever. The days of the Caesars and the dictators; of the terrorists and the assassins are already numbered.

It will be decisive and righteous (v. 18), for God's reign will set right the scales at last, judging the rebellious and rewarding the obedient, whether small or great.

The Christian reader should allow this wonderful picture to control mind and heart. Let us look forward to the eternal Reign, but let us also anticipate it in our churches and hasten it in our neighbourhoods! I mentioned All Souls Church. All around that church are the representatives of many nations. Regent Street is full of them. But inside, and gathered at the table of the Holy Communion, many nations are present – English, American, Chinese, Asian and African – bonded together in one family and under one King. An anticipation of the future! Then, from the centre, the fellowship fans out once more into the restless city, to work, to witness ... and to hasten the kingdom that will last for ever.

The seven trumpets of warning judgements are over. They close in verse 19 with the vision of God's sanctuary, and with the reminder (in the ark of the covenant) of his faithfulness to his people.

Or have we bumped into the beginning of the next section?

Wilcock suggests this in his commentary. We may be like the man who has stayed seated in the cinema when the film is already over. Without knowing it he is seeing the start of the next film! With verse 19, the titles are already going up for the heart and core of the Apocalypse – The Victory of the Lamb.

SUGGESTIONS FOR STUDY

Read on your own chapters 8–11 of the Revelation. Then in your own study or fellowship group, you may wish to read and discuss chapter 11:1-13. The following questions may help to stimulate thinking:

1. Consider the 'trampling' of verse 2. In what way has this been taking place? Can the group members think of definite instances?

2. Can someone in the group summarize what is indicated by this period of forty-two months, or 1,260 days? What is the significance of it for Christian work today?

3. Who or what are the two witnesses? Where does their power come from, and what is their historical role? How far can you identify with them?

4. Without too much discussion (yet) on the beast of verse 7, consider how John's first readers of the Revelation might have identified this being. How many in the group were aware of a degree of opposition when they first began to take Christian discipleship seriously? What form did it take, and how can you encourage one another by your experiences?

5. Might there be a tendency for some readers of the Revelation to fall into a determinist view of the book – to give way to a passive fatalism about the beast, for example? Where is the flaw in this kind of thinking?

6. What encourages you most in this passage? What alarms or challenges you most?

7. How do you interpret verses 11-13? What principles and conclusions may we draw?

PART FOUR

THE VICTORY OF THE LAMB

'I have often sat down with wonder and delight, and admired how God made the very schemes which his enemies contrived, in order to hinder, become the most effectual means to propagate his gospel ... The seed of the woman shall bruise the serpent's head. Fear not men. Be not too much cast down at the deceitfulness of your hearts. Fear not devils; you shall get the victory even over them. The Lord Jesus has engaged to make you more than conquerors over all.'

From a sermon by George Whitefield
(By courtesy of The Banner of Truth Trust)

10

BATTLE WITH SATAN

Years ago I was playing in a schoolboys' tennis event in London. We were at the famous All England Club in Wimbledon, competing for a shiny trophy called the Youll Cup. Each school was represented by two doubles pairs – the idea being that if the score levelled at one match apiece, a deciding singles would settle the tie and the entry into the next round.

I shall never forget the winning school team. It possessed only one quality player – but he was already an international! Consequently, in round after round the story repeated itself. Dominating the court, he would keep his highly vulnerable partner well protected from all harm; the second pair invariably crumbled; then in the singles play-off, the international would cruise comfortably to victory and pull his team through to the next round. Our own team fell to him in the semi-final.

A one-man victory! So it seemed to the rest of us, as the cup was solemnly handed to the lucky winners at the end. Off they marched – including the incompetent second pair – clutching the trophy that they hardly seemed to deserve. But they were the winners.

Look at Revelation 12:11 for a similar description of the frail Church of God in its battle against the wiles of the Devil:

'They overcame him.'

They ... a miserable bunch of accused nonentities in the mighty Roman Empire, driven into the catacombs, thrown into the arena. And whom did they overcome? This chapter describes their superhuman foe in various terms. He is the *dragon* (v. 7), therefore very powerful; he is the *serpent* (v. 9), therefore very cunning; he is the *devil* (v. 9), therefore a 'slanderer'; he is *Satan* (v. 9), therefore the 'adversary' (see Zech. 3:1); and he is the *accuser* (v. 10), therefore full of deceit.

The Church against the devil – it's hardly a fair line-up. And yet ... and yet ... *the Church overcomes!* So thunders the message of Revelation. Christians everywhere have always loved this central chapter, which forms the very heart of the Apocalypse. Once again we are looking at another 'parallel' view of the entire era spanned by our Lord's first and second comings. So far, we have been looking largely at the outward patterns and events surfacing in the story of the Church. Now, in a more definite way, we are introduced to the unseen spiritual conflict that lies behind our world's struggles.

John's readers in Asia Minor were to learn that theirs was not simply the battle of a minor religious community to resist the harassment of an imperialist regime. It was all part of the ongoing conflict between the divine and the demonic, between the higher and the fallen powers, between light and darkness.

Not that the light and darkness are co-equal. The Bible never teaches dualism. Satan – a fallen angel, and therefore a created being – has no independent existence, and is certainly not on a par with the Creator. In this sense he can even be termed, as Luther called him, 'God's devil.' He has chosen to be in rebellion – a rebellion which affects both the physical and the spiritual realm. But the rebellion is going to be ended!

The process has already started. Follow the course of the battle with Satan, as our chapter traces it.

The dragon frustrated (12:1-6)

As you read this section, do the pieces begin to fit into place – the woman and the dragon, the birth of the male child, the threats, the snatching of the child up to heaven and the pursuit of the woman into the wilderness? Think about it a moment.

The dragon we have already identified as the devil, the enemy of God and his people. The woman is the Church – though originally she would have been Israel. The sun, moon and stars of verse 1 are a flash-back to Genesis 37:9, where the children of Israel were portrayed by these symbols, in Joseph's dream.

So the woman represents the people of God – and it is she who gives birth to the male child. How painful the process was! Think of all that Israel went through in the Old Testament – the bondage in Egypt, the wanderings, the exile. These were the birth-pangs (v. 2) that preceded the coming of the Messiah. Many were the attempts to frustrate the plan of God, both before and after the birth of Jesus. Herod was to make his attempts early on in the Gospel narrative. Behind such attempts lay the evil designs of the powerful dragon; powerful, but not *all*-powerful (notice the limitation of the 'third' in verse 4).

The momentum increases as Jesus begins his ministry and makes his assault upon the strongholds of death and the demon world. It is a collision course. It culminates at a place of execution outside Israel's capital over a dramatic weekend. Tragedy strikes; the Messiah is dead. The darkness sweeps in and the dragon has won.... *No, he hasn't!*

'And her child was snatched up to God and to his throne' (12:5).

Have you got the interpretation? Yes, it is the triumphant ascension of Jesus that we read about here.

> The Cross completed his saving work.
> The Resurrection confirmed it.
> The Ascension celebrated it.
> The dragon had been frustrated.

Even so, the way is never easy for God's people. The woman is under pressure now, out in the wilderness. Have you felt this at times? The solitude of your Christian position; the pressure; the adversity? *It is very biblical to feel this.* We may take courage also, because we learn from verse 6 that the woman is taken care of, out there in the wilderness, for a period of ... how long?

1,260 days. It's the Elijah period again (11:3); the period of being fed and maintained in the wilderness, the period of power and authority for God's people, the era when we may expect things to happen! At times it seemed as though the light was to be extinguished. Persecution, false teaching and godless materialism have taken their toll in every century. But somehow it seems that the frail Church, with all its human failings, is destined to survive its wilderness ordeal and to overcome.

The dragon has been frustrated, and will continue to be frustrated.

The dragon expelled (12:7-12)
'And there was war in heaven....' Don't read this chronologically – or geographically! We are looking at the video recording of the winning goal all over again – but from a different camera position. Here we are seeing the effect of the historical death of Jesus Christ upon the unseen spiritual realm. While

the event of the Cross was taking place in Jerusalem – visible to the eyes of soldiers and passers-by – an *invisible* conflict was being concluded in the angelic sphere, hence the reference to 'Michael and his angels' in verse 7.

Difficult? Not really. The prophecies in Daniel help us here, because they portray a being called Michael, as appearing on several occasions as defender of God's people against their enemies. 'At that time Michael, the great prince who protects your people, will arise' (Dan. 12:1).

Sir Jacob Epstein's wonderful sculpture outside England's Coventry Cathedral depicts the victory of Michael over the dragon. I have often gazed at this superb symbol of our victory in Christ, and have felt a renewal of inspiration and courage.

May this passage lift every reader whose confidence has been sapped or whose faith has been eroded. Reminder after glorious reminder comes reverberating through these pages to assure us that Jesus Christ is the great Winner, and that death, darkness and despair are the great Losers!

'They overcame him by the blood of the Lamb' (v. 11).

There is the ground of our assurance. We may understand the victory in terms of the *cosmic*, for ultimately it was a spiritual conflict. But we must also understand it in terms of the *historic*. There is nothing phantom-like about 'blood'; our victory in Christ is grounded in an event. We may also understand the victory of the Cross in terms of the *dynamic*, for it actually makes a difference that Christ has won. Christians should never think of themselves as those working towards victory. Rather, they are those who work and witness for God *from* the position of victory already achieved! This puts a different complexion upon everything.

'But,' you say, 'if the devil is already the loser, why does he still seem so powerful? We see him at work everywhere in our world.' By way of answer I refer you to the third section of this chapter.

The dragon enraged (12:12-17)

Look at these sentences, and you will see that the overthrow of Satan and his expulsion from the heavenly battlefield had decided his fate. His days are numbered; 'his time is short' (v. 12). His is the situation of the dictator who has been ousted from his capital. His centre has gone and his next stop will be the border! But woe betide anyone who gets in his way meanwhile, for – although defeated – he is still a dangerous foe, and he has not admitted his defeat.

I remember playing Monopoly against my wife. 'Go on, give up!' she would say, when she had gained virtually the whole board. But in my stubborn male pride I would refuse to let go. 'No, no, we'll go on until the end.' In my heart, however, I would know that I was doomed.

If we may say it reverently, God has the whole board. He has the green lot, the brown lot, the yellow lot, Mayfair and Park Lane! The opposition has been dispossessed, except perhaps for one miserable mortgaged station and the water works. The opposition has not given up, however. It is battling on until the very last move, till Armageddon, till the End.

This is why we find ourselves to be locked in battle, still. But it is Calvary – and Easter – that tell us we are on the winning side, that assure us that if we resist the devil he will flee from us (James 4:7). A follower of Jesus Christ need not give way to temptation. When we belong to him, we have the power to say 'No' to evil. If we fall, it is because our motivation is weak, to the extent that we don't even *want* to win. The secret of making progress in character and lifestyle is to enlarge the vision that we have of Jesus Christ. As we do this, through Scripture meditation, through prayer, through the Holy Communion and the Church fellowship, so our desire increases. Then, to our amazement, we find that we can beat down Satan under our feet!

There is no need to be surprised about the pressure of Christian living. It is a sure sign that we are related to Christ if we are aware of temptation and conflict. By trusting in Christ, we invite upon ourselves the attention of Christ's adversary. But we ride upon eagles' wings (verse 14 – a reference to Exodus 19:4), and we are secure for a period of … how long?

'… a time, times and half a time' (v. 14).

How long do you think 'a time' signifies? Could it be a year? And how long is 'times'? Two years conceivably? And 'half a time' – yes, you're already there; it adds up to three and a half years, or 1,260 days! Elijah once again is the illustration of our Christian era of advance and expectation of victory in Christ. When we pray in the name of Jesus we should expect things to happen. When in his power we confront temptation, our adversary has no other option but to retreat!

The fight for moral victory in our lives is never easy. To represent Christ's cause in an alien society is no balloon-ride. But at least we stand with Calvary and Easter behind us. Satan has some power against us, but it is limited. The tempter can only *tempt* – he cannot force us to go his way; he is on his way out. No matter if the concept of a personal devil is difficult to grasp. In a sermon on the devil, Alec Vidler put it well once: 'What you have got to do is not define him, but renounce him!'

For your reading
Revelation, chapter 12.

11

ALLIES OF SATAN

Somebody once asked me over lunch which notorious men of history I would select for an all-time football team of evil. Perhaps you have indulged in frivolous exercises like this yourself ... Idi Amin in goal ... Hitler in an attacking position ... and so on. In any list built up, surely several names present themselves from the time of the Roman Empire. Tiberius, Caligula, Nero, Domitian ... the names spill out effortlessly.

It was no game for those early Christians. The period of the Revelation was a time of intense pressure for the Faith. The Roman Caesar was like an immovable mountain – no, he wasn't, he was like a beast! Combine the ferocity of a leopard with the power of a bear; mix that with the terror of a lion and invest the resulting horror with the evil of the dragon, and there you have it, reports John in his famous chapter 13. Or perhaps you haven't even then, because the beast is reported to have ten horns and seven heads!

Let's go 'preterist' for a moment and relate the prophecy specifically to the time at which it was written. It wasn't hard for John's readers to see in the *beast* almost a code-word for the emperor. He seemed, in his blasphemous and ferocious rule, to be virtually indestructible. True, Nero was out of the picture by now – he had committed suicide on a June day in AD 68. But the beast was a little like the Hydra of Aesop's fables. Remove a head, and another grows in its place!

'One of the heads of the beast seemed to have had a fatal wound, but the fatal wound had been healed' (13:3).

Could John have been referring to Nero? Or conceivably to the disastrous year of AD 69, when three contestants occupied the imperial throne in rapid succession? At any rate, seven major figures since Augustus had been the objects of Caesar-worship; on this interpretation they would appear to be the seven heads of verse 1 – each with a blasphemous name. As a matter of fact, Nero, on his coins, was titled *Saviour of the World*. Domitian was addressed as *Dominus et Deus noster* ('Our lord and god').

The ten horns and crowns point to the completeness of the beast's power and authority. It was impossible to make war against him (v. 4) – the line of emperors looked like going on for ever.

Let's go 'historicist' for a moment. Could this be a sort of history written in advance? Could people living in later generations claim, with justification, to identify the beast? The attempts have certainly been made! Candidates have ranged from various dictatorships and empires to some of history's less impressive church leaders. It seems unwise to make specific pronouncements, however. It is enough to say that the beast is something of a political animal. Its very origin suggests this, for *the sea* (v. 1) appears – in its surging restlessness – to be associated in the Bible with nations, peoples and governments (Isa. 17:12; Rev. 17:15). The language is reminiscent of the vision of the four beasts in Daniel chapter 7. These were certainly political (Dan. 7:17).

History has repeatedly and predictably produced governments that have thrived on naked power, opposing God and threatening his people. The historicists have a point.

Let's go 'parallelist' for a moment. Is this ascendancy of the beast from the sea a definite characteristic of the Gospel age in which we are now living? The answer seems to be 'Yes.'

'The beast was given a mouth to utter proud words and blasphemies and to exercise his authority for forty-two months' (v. 5).

Elijah once again! The forty-two months of this prophet's period of authoritative power were marked by great signs and wonders; but it was also a period of intense conflict. If Elijah's three and a half years are to be taken as a picture of our own Christian era, then we too must expect conflict to accompany every success and spiritual advance. At times it may seem worse than others. Dietrich Bonhoffer, whose sturdy defiance of the Hitler regime led to his own death at a concentration camp in 1945, wrote prophetically:

'The messengers of Jesus will be hated to the end of time. They will be blamed for all the divisions which rend cities and homes. Jesus and his disciples will be condemned on all sides for undermining family life, and for leading the nation astray; they will be called crazy fanatics and disturbers of the peace' *(The Cost of Discipleship, SCM Press, 1959).*

In general we find that governments, in our period spanned by the birth and the return of Christ, have not readily welcomed the voice of a renewed and witnessing Church. Again I quote – this time from Sir Frederick Catherwood: 'In most countries in the world the Christian has about as much chance of becoming a part of government as Peter had of replacing Pontius Pilate, or Paul had of replacing Festus or Felix.'

Let's go 'futurist' for a moment. Is this figure of the beast to become a world ruler at the end time? The text suggests it:

> 'And he was given authority over every tribe, people, language and nation. All inhabitants of the earth will worship the beast – all whose names have not been written in the book of life belonging to the Lamb that was slain from the creation of the world' (vv. 7, 8).

A person? An institution? A machine? ... To be honest, I am wary of some of the more sensational interpretations around today. And I am suspicious of the judgemental theology that writes off a society as beyond redemption, in the belief that the End is near; I am somewhat sceptical of the scaremongers who identify the United Nations or the EEC computer at Brussels ... or anything, as the beast. And I run a mile from certain so-called prophets of our time who have escaped to their own self-created wildernesses, there to wail that they are the only true remnant of God left. Let them stay in their wildernesses if they must. But the rest of us have an urgent task to fulfil for the kingdom of God!

This being accepted, however, there is enough of an indication in Scripture to prepare us for a threefold development:

A long period – the 'three and a half years' of our present Christian era.

A short period – the 'three and a half days' (11:9) of unsurpassed evil.

The End itself, and the triumph of God (11:11).

The call upon us is not for guess-work or speculation, but for 'patient endurance and faithfulness' (3:10), regardless of what period we may think we are living in.

The beast. He may be a personification of evil – a counterfeit of the Incarnation – or the term may be a figurative one for a government or institution. Elsewhere we read of antichrist (1 John 2:18, 22; 4:3; 2 John 7), a being that supposedly takes the place of Christ, in opposition to his rule. In 2 Thessalonians 2:3 there is reference to the coming of 'the man of lawlessness'. All these seem to be different ways of expressing a single truth. But wait! What is this we see now?

'Then I saw another beast, coming out of the earth' (13:11).

It seems superfluous, coming after the evils of which we have just read – but there we have it. *Another beast!* What does it represent? The interpretation is not too difficult. Whereas the first beast is the *secular* ally of Satan, the second beast is the *religious*. It masquerades as the Lamb (v. 11), but it speaks like a dragon. It speaks on behalf of the first beast and in that sense is its public relations officer, as Professor F. F. Bruce has suggested. Later in the Apocalypse, it is described as the false prophet (16:13).

Have you come up against false religion? Almost certainly you have. John's first readers may have been vulnerable to the imperial priesthood in their own time. Such religion would have presented the way of compromise: 'Take it easy, no need to make martyrs of yourselves; show a little respect to the emperor as Lord – it's only a form of words.' *Ease up!*

But at times in Christian history the Church has become dead and cold. Doctrine has become dry, and the flame of love and worship has flickered out. In this case false religion makes the believer *freeze up.*

Alternatively, the flames of worship and enthusiasm can flare so brightly that they have the effect of tipping the Christian community towards sectarianism and extremism, until in the end we simply *seize up!* Any method will do if Christ's followers can only be seduced from their first love and come under the control of another.

Is this not what verse 16 is hinting at? We do not have to look for literal 'marks' on right hand or forehead to identify followers of the beast. It is when people's *actions* (the right hand) and *thinking* (the forehead) are controlled by a philosophy alien to Christ, that you could say the beast has stamped himself upon their lives.

And the number of the beast? Oh the theories that have been advanced about the number 666! Surely the clue lies within the passage itself:

> 'If anyone has insight, let him calculate the number of the beast, for it is man's number. His number is 666' (v. 18).

Man's number – for man was created on the sixth day, if you recall.

I like Hendriksen's comment in his *More than Conquerors* (Tyndale Press): 'Six, moreover, is not seven and never reaches seven. It always fails to attain to perfection; that is, it never becomes seven. Six means missing the mark, or failure. Seven means perfection or victory. Rejoice, O Church of God! The victory is on your side. The number of the beast is 666, that is, failure upon failure upon failure! It is the number of man, for the beast glories in man; and must fail!'

* * *

God is our strength and refuge,
our present help in trouble;
and we therefore will not fear,
though the earth should change!
Though mountains shake and tremble,
though swirling floods are raging,
God the Lord of hosts is with us evermore!

There is a flowing river,
within God's holy city;
God is in the midst of her –
she shall not be moved!
God's help is swiftly given,
thrones vanish at his presence –
God the Lord of hosts is with us evermore!

Come, see the works of our maker,
learn of his deeds all-powerful;
wars will cease across the world
when he shatters the spear!
Be still and know your creator,
uplift him in the nations –
God the Lord of hosts is with us evermore!

© Richard Bewes, Jubilate Hymns.
Tune: The Dambusters March, by Eric Coates.

For your reading
Revelation, chapter 13.

12

THE GREAT DIVIDE

'I see that Donald Maclean is dead.'

It was a Saturday morning as I scanned the newspaper headlines featuring the death of a man notorious for his involvement in the Spy of the Century scandal. I was staying with my father on England's south coast at the time.

Dad looked up from his breakfast coffee. 'Yes, I'd heard it on the news. I used to know Donald Maclean.'

'You knew him?' I had never heard this before.

'Yes, I've got his picture in an album.'

Presently I was looking at a faded snapshot portraying a small, excited bunch of teenage boys on an English beach. The details were pointed out to me.

As a student, Dad had been leading a 'beach mission' at Southwold, in the English county of Suffolk. In the centre of the group was a bright-faced young lad. That was Donald Maclean. He had been encouraged to attend the Christian mission by his father, Sir Donald Maclean. On young Donald's right was a face I thought I recognized. It belonged to Quintin Carr who was to become, years later, a prominent Christian communicator to youth. On Donald's left was another face I vaguely recognized.

'You know him,' confirmed Dad. 'Herbert Taylor's his name.'

I nodded. Herbert Taylor had become an outstanding clergyman and founder of the well-known Pathfinder movement. Now he was in retirement. A third face – just behind Donald's – intrigued me.

'You know him, too,' declared Dad. 'You remember Clarence Foster?'

'Of course.' Clarence Foster had gone on to become one of the leading lights in the annual Christian convention held at Keswick, with an influence that was international.

'So Donald Maclean had at least a flirtation with Christianity,' I commented. 'Whatever happened to him?'

We shall never know precisely. Did Maclean retain something of what he heard at Southwold in 1925? What were the forces that he allowed to govern his career – a career that ended in the lonely alcoholism of a flat in Moscow? Whatever the details, he took a path far removed from that of his contemporaries in the beach mission.

We can never solve the imponderables of the 'grey areas' of life, and it is not in our province to pronounce where people may or may not be in their relationship to Jesus Christ. What the Bible does – and this is no less true of the book of Revelation – is to highlight the stark, the ultimate issues.

For in the end there are only two groups. Read about them in chapter 14 of the Apocalypse:

'And they sang a new song before the throne and before the four living creatures and the elders. No-one could learn the song except the 144,000 who had been redeemed from the earth.... They follow the Lamb wherever he goes .... And the smoke of their torment rises for ever and ever. There is no rest day or night for those who worship the beast and his image, or for anyone who receives the mark of his name ...' (14:3, 4, 11).

The message is a sobering one. You can take any group of people and – invisibly – there will be a line drawn down the middle. Some are going to go God's way. Others will go their own way, and in so doing identify themselves with the opposition; in short, with the beast.

The contrast is strong. On the one side of the divide we survey the followers of the Lamb, the 144,000 (14:1). On the other side are the worshippers of the beast. Between these two groups is the voice of the eternal gospel (vv. 6,7). And at the end of the road is 'The harvest of the earth' (vv. 14-20), the judgement.

Meditate on the contrast. The Lamb's followers have a new song to sing; the beast's have no rest. The Lamb's followers are sealed with God's name on their foreheads, safe for eternity; the beast's are branded with his mark. The Lamb's followers are safe, 'purchased from among men' (v. 4); the beast's are vulnerable and heading for the fall associated with Babylon (v. 8). The Lamb's followers are, through the Gospel, visualized as pure (vv. 4, 5); the beast's are tainted with Babylon's adulteries (v. 8). The Lamb's followers follow him into happiness (vv. 4, 13); the beast's are heading towards the judgement (vv. 10, 11, 14-20).

The encouragement for believers comes in verse 12 of this chapter!

This calls for patient endurance on the part of the saints who obey God's commandments and remain faithful to Jesus.

Chapter 14 gives us the true perspective in our world of buffeting hostilities. For what we see around us, in our present disturbed scene, are not the pulsating vibrations of a kingdom in ascendancy. They are the thrashing death-throes of a kingdom in desperation!

Which way will we choose? Seen in this light, there is no hesitation for most people. We want to go the way of purity, of harmony and truth. But the choice doesn't usually present itself like this! The issue normally faces us in a multiplicity of tiny and perfectly natural decisions: *How shall I spend the Easter week-end? ... Which group shall I identify with at my new college? ... Shall I compromise with this shady business deal just this once? ...*

When the judgement finally comes, it will only serve as an underlying of the decisions that we have been making all our life. Not that we cannot effect a change-over. The penitent thief is our classic example. That is the incredible mercy of God; even at the last minute he will forgive and accept a repentant individual who has repeatedly shut the door in the face of Christ.

A woman once wrote to me after a talk on television:

'Since I have spent a lifetime calling myself an agnostic, it hardly seems worth changing my label on the last lap.'

Of course I encouraged her to change! There is still time. The final harvest is yet to come. And in the light of this chapter, who would not wish to take careful steps, on a daily basis, to identify with the Lamb and his followers?

SUGGESTIONS FOR STUDY

Read on your own chapters 12–14 of the Apocalypse. Subsequently in a study group, you may wish to concentrate on chapter 12. Let the following questions help your discussion:

1. How difficult have members of the group found it to conceive of a personal devil who works in opposition to

God? Why do some people find this difficult? Examine these passages for further light – 2 Corinthians 11:14; 2 Thessalonians 2:9.

2. Trace the sequence depicted in verses 1-6. Can you describe in your own words what is portrayed here?

3. 'A woman' (v. 1). How far is this an apt symbol of the Church of God? How does it match up with today's image?

4. Read verses 7-12. How do you interpret the concept of 'war in heaven'?

5. What is the main point made in verses 7-12? What sentences or phrases particularly highlight the central truth?

6. What should be the Christian's principal attitude towards spiritual conflict?

7. How far do you identify with the position of the woman in verses 13-17?

PART FIVE

THE OVERTHROW OF EVIL

'The Christian who pays attention to the New Testament records is not likely to be deluded by utopian expectations of the future. He knows that good and evil grow together, and will do so until the time of the end. He knows that evil, cast forth in one form, displays the utmost ingenuity in transforming itself and finding its way back in another. He knows that the Kingdom of God will not come upon earth until God Himself is pleased to bring it by a new act of His sovereign power.'

Stephen Neill,
Christian Faith Today
(Penguin Books)

13

THE ROAD TO ARMAGEDDON

I recall seeing an item in a newspaper which carried the headline, 'Butler dusted deadly bomb for 24 years.' It was a German bomb that had been dropped in World War Two, within the grounds of seventeenth-century Belton House, near Grantham in Lincolnshire. It was the home of Lord and Lady Brownlow.

The daily dust and polish was given to the bomb by the butler, Charles Patience. One day he even dropped it on his foot! But a visiting army officer, one Easter week-end, identified the bomb as live and dangerous. A Royal Air Force bomb disposal unit was called in, and the thing was eventually disposed of.

You can live with danger, without realizing it. You can even delude yourself into believing that you are indestructible, and that things will go on for ever as they are. It takes an expert analyst – or an apocalypse – to persuade us towards another view.

For this is what the book of Revelation is for. It is not given to satisfy our curiosity, but to open our eyes, to prod us into wakefulness and to stimulate action – and reform.

We read now of the seven bowls (chs. 15 and 16), with their portrayal of God's final judgement. No, we are not contemplating the last, universal and ultimate judgement here. What we are being warned of is the approach of judgements in history that are final in their nature, with no redress. Earlier, in Revelation chapters 8–11, we were reading of the *warning* trumpets of judgement, sounded in order to lead people to repentance.

But what of those who harden their consciences and follow the beast? In such a case, God's final judgements are sent (final, but not complete until the last day).

The totality of the judgements (15:1)

These are 'last' plagues (v. 1) because 'with them God's wrath is completed'. Chapter 16 suggests they take the form of events that bring someone's life to an end. At that point there can be no further appeal and no intercession (we learn that no one can enter the temple – i.e. to pray – until the judgements are complete, 15:8).

I find Wilcock's commentary convincing here:

'Whenever destruction comes upon the impenitent sinner, there is, for him, the 'last day', the end of his world, and the final confrontation with Christ, who comes at all times like a thief, when men least expect him.'

The familiarity of the judgements (15:2-4)

As we read these sentences, we can sense history repeating itself. The judgements are described as 'plagues'; the victorious believers are depicted standing by a sea, and they are singing 'the song of Moses the servant of God and the song of the Lamb.'

It's the Red Sea all over again – but telescoped with our own Christian era. The American slaves in the cotton plantations had the knack of linking Old Testament and New Testament themes in a similar way:

O Mary, don't you weep, don't you mourn,
O Mary, don't weep, don't mourn;
Pharaoh's army was drowned,
O Mary, don't weep.

Pharaoh indeed learnt to his cost that you cannot perpetually keep God on the end of a string. Our familiarity with this theme of judgement ought to prepare us to find it strongly to the fore in the Revelation.

The purity of the judgements (15:5-8)
We have seen the Tabernacle earlier, in 11:19. Now we see it again, although in a different context. The wrath of which we read here is divine, holy and utterly pure.

In the last analysis, no one is going to complain about the justice of God. No one will ever say, 'Oh, it wasn't fair; I had no chance.' God's judgement is not accidental or capricious. Even Judas Iscariot, on facing the facts of his guilt, admitted, 'I have betrayed innocent blood.' He knew, all right.

The variety of the judgements (16:1-21)
In chapter 16, we see the different bowls described – and they form an interesting parallel with the seven trumpets of chapters 8–11. We read of *incurable diseases* (v. 2 – a reminder of the plague of boils in Exodus chapter 9). We read of *sea disasters* (v. 3), of *calamities on inland rivers* (vv. 4-7), and of *drought and scorching* (vv. 8, 9).

We read of the beast's throne and kingdom being plunged into *darkness* in verse 10 (reminiscent of Egypt's darkness of Exodus 10). Finally we read of the *final battle* (of Armageddon, vv. 12-16), and of the *day of judgement* (vv. 17-21).

A few points need to be made clear. Are all people who are struck by disease under the judgement of God? Or, for that matter, people in countries plagued by drought? The answer must be No. Of course we all die one day. It is possible that, in certain countries, drought is the actual means by which someone's life is terminated. In another country it might be an environmental disease. And what might for *some* be a catastrophe that brings them to the judgement of God, will for *others* simply be the gateway to the life with Christ that lies beyond the grave. We must be thankful that it is God who is the judge, and none other.

A second point: what is Armageddon? *Symbolically* it stands for the final collision between good and evil. *Geographically*, it would have been Megiddo, situated about twenty miles south-west of Nazareth. It is, indeed, a traditional battlefield. It was probably the site of the battle of the Kishon River (Judg. 4:13-16 – compare Judg. 5:19) between Sisera and Barak. There Sisera's chariot wheels became stuck in the mud. Napoleon defeated the Turkish army at the same spot on 16th April 1799 (the Turks also got bogged down in the mud). General Allenby also fought there in 1917.

As it is pictured here in 16:12-16, Armageddon represents the climactic convergence of the powers of good and evil. The three unclean spirits (vv. 13, 14) would seem to represent demonic influences unleashed upon that day. This is the same event as that portrayed in 20:7-10. In that passage, God's camp is seen as being surrounded and on the point of defeat, before a dramatic divine intervention that reverses the fortunes. Is this then the 'short period' of three and a half days (11:11, 12)? I think so. Armageddon, then, will simply usher in the final day of judgement, on which we read of Babylon, the citadel of evil, falling apart in ruins.

Does it all seem somewhat unreal? We should be prepared. No one can say we are without warning.

I well remember inviting someone to supper, some years ago. All would have been well, if only I had remembered to tell my wife. As it was, the bell rang – and there was the unexpected guest. It was like a judgement upon me. Just a simple little supper, we had said to each other earlier. A cosy little meal for two – just a boiled egg and a banana. And then …!

The road to Armageddon. Every day brings us all a little nearer to that appointment. And some of us sooner than others.

For your reading
Revelation, chapters 15 and 16.

14

THE MYSTERY WOMAN

You can get too clever with the book of Revelation. The vision was intended to comfort and prepare us, not to test our ingenuity. As we come to chapters 17 and 18, we are introduced to a new figure, that of a woman. But she stands in strong contrast to the woman of chapter 12, already identified as the Church. There is a mystery about her, and it is proclaimed in her title (17:5):

MYSTERY
BABYLON THE GREAT
THE MOTHER OF PROSTITUTES
AND OF THE ABOMINATIONS OF THE EARTH

Let's not get too clever. It is possible to plunge into the extravagant imagery of these chapters, to come up with an impressive display of nimble and even convincing explanations and to think that you have then 'solved' the mystery of the woman astride the scarlet beast, together with the seven heads, seven hills, seven kings, Babylon and the rest.

It isn't that I disagree with the findings of the Bible commentators. At least ... not exactly! I can nod sagely when told that the seven kings (17:9, 10) represent the seven anti-Christian empires of Ancient Babylonia, Assyria, New Babylonia, Medo-Persia, Greco-Macedonia, Rome and finally all other such empires rolled into one. I nod again when I learn from another source that they represent the seven Caesars – Augustus, Tiberius, Caligula, Claudius, Nero, Vespasian and Titus.

But then I wonder what this would all mean to a Bible reader in the Amazon basin, or to a new believer whose historical knowledge is restricted to that of the Ming dynasties of China? Is it essential for them to bone up on the history of Europe in order to make sense of Revelation 17 and 18? Or will a working knowledge of the Bible alone provide sufficient guidance?

Take the ten kings of 17:12. I read this in one commentary: 'Many writers identify them as Parthian satraps coming from the east in a massive invasion under the leadership of a revived Nero.... Still others take them to be the governors of senatorial provinces who held office for one year.' A less equipped but nevertheless popular writer identifies the ten kings with the European Economic Community! Is it any wonder that ordinary readers of the Bible can feel defeated when approaching the book of Revelation? Let the mystery woman remain a mystery, we tend to mutter, as we put on the coffee.

No, don't give up! Remember, these are *visions*, not brain-teasers. And when the Bible speaks about a 'mystery', it is encouraging to learn that the mystery remains so only to the outsiders, never to the initiated. To those who have made a beginning as Christian disciples, the secrets of God's disclosures are secrets no longer. They are an open secret. The apostle Paul once wrote:

> '... you will be able to understand my insight into the mystery of Christ, which was not made known to men in other generations ... ' (Eph. 3:4, 5).

So what of this mystery woman? Let us not despise the commentators for one moment, but let us nevertheless read chapters 17 and 18 for ourselves, thoughtfully, prayerfully. See these vivid images as you would watch a screened display of colour transparencies, where one picture dissolves into the next, only to be followed by further projection, and then another....

Then sift and analyse your impressions. Do it now – and then let us compare our findings!

* * *

Something must have come across to you. The pride of this woman? Her flashy appearance? Her opposition to the saints? Her alliance with the beast? Her destined fate? The main features of these chapters will become evident to those already enlightened by the Spirit of Christ. About this woman we learn:

The revealed mystery of her identity (17:1-6)
It's all there – if we have eyes to see it. The mystery woman represents worldly power in all its seductive fascination. She is seen in two guises – as an immoral woman, and as a wicked city.

Babylon ... Featuring as early as Genesis 10:10 (a city built by Nimrod), Babylon represents one of the early cities of the world – and undoubtedly the proudest. It may have been linked with the tower at Babel (Gen. 11), equally a symbol of the pride of godless men. In time, Babylon came to stand for all that opposed the people of God and pandered to the vanities of egotistical rulers such as Nebuchadnezzar:

> 'Is not this the great Babylon I have built as the royal residence, by my mighty power and for the glory of my majesty?' (Dan. 4:30).

Glittering, power-obsessed, worshipping 'everything in the world – the cravings of sinful man, the lust of his eyes and the boasting of what he has and does' (1 John 2:16), this is the great harlot of Revelation; this is the wicked city of Babylon.

We have been up against her all along, in her attempt to seduce us from what is just and pure. She offers so much from her golden cup (17:4) – popularity, wealth, ease and promotion; but there is no lasting satisfaction to be had from her. Lord Byron described his own experience graphically: 'Drank every cup of joy, drank draughts which common millions might have drunk. Then died of thirst, because there was no more to drink.'

There is nothing to be had from Babylon. We are actually at war with the way of life she represents (17:6). But did you notice a second facet of the mystery woman?

The familiar mystery of her power (17:6-14)
'Why are you astonished?' asks the angel of John (17:7). The apostle was recoiling with amazement at the vision of the woman – but he need not have done so. Part of the vision, at least, was familiar – for the woman is riding upon a being that has already been introduced:

> 'The beast, which you saw, once was, now is not, and will come up out of the Abyss and go to his destruction' (17:8).

Yes, it is the beast coming out of the sea that the woman Babylon is allied to. With his seven heads (v. 9 – the essence of secular authority and rule), and with his ten horns, and blasphemous names, he is very powerful. Image merges into image here – the seven heads are seven hills (John would immediately have thought of Rome, with its seven hills). Look again – and you will see that they are seven kings (v. 9). Add to those the ten horns of verse 12 – which appear to represent anti-Christian governments of the future, complete ('ten') with their accumulation of authoritative (though limited – 'one hour') power; and we have a fairly composite picture. *It is a concentration of power that will make war against the Lamb throughout history* (v. 14). Many tyrannical regimes have already risen, only to go down into oblivion; surely this is the sense conveyed by the reminder that several kings have already fallen (v. 10). As each one falls, the civilized world sighs with relief. Now, surely, things will get better! That may be, but the relief is only temporary. *It is a familiar pattern*, for we can recall an earlier statement: 'One of the heads of the beast seemed to have had a fatal wound, but the fatal wound had been healed' (13:3).

This is the power that undergirds the harlot, Babylon. The alliance is not permanent, however. Read on!

The surprise mystery of her fragility (17:15-18)
How very influential is seductive, attractive Babylon! And yet she is only a pack of cards. Take any great city of the modern world – San Francisco ... Nairobi ... Buenos Aires. It only takes a financial crisis, a power black-out or a change of government for the whole veneer of civilized behaviour to crack. Let the lights go out for only a little while, and the looters will soon come swarming out. Such stability as our urbanized society possesses is owed almost entirely to its tenuous links with Christian norms and standards.

Babylon is very fragile. The end of chapter 17 shows the secular power turning upon her (v. 16). Is this surprising? It ought not to be! Is it not the way of totalitarian regimes to sweep into power with worldly inducements? Bread ... circuses

... reduced income tax ... greater freedom? But once into power, the promised bonanza tends to evaporate into thin air. Babylon is only a harlot, and is cynically used as such! Now look on at chapter 18 for a last look at the woman.

The ultimate mystery of her desolation (ch. 18)
The warning could hardly be stronger. If you centre your energies and hopes in a philosophy that limits life to possessions, position and pleasure, you are going to be overthrown!

Babylon was always the symbol of power-crazed worldliness, second-rate in its objectives and doomed to destruction. Here is a mystery of the Bible, but it is a revealed mystery for those with eyes to see. Read Isaiah 13:19-22; 21:9, and Jeremiah 51:6-9, and you will see that John's vision of collapsing Babylon was no new concept.

The themes of Revelation 18 are easy to pick out. *There is certainty here* (vv. 1-3); the language is that of the 'prophetic past' – Babylon has already fallen, so certain is the coming event. *There is warning here* (vv. 4, 5), for God's people are told to keep their distance, lest they become entangled in Babylon's sins, and thus in her downfall. *There is retribution here* (vv. 5-8); no tears are to be shed when the harlot's demise is announced. *There is disillusionment here* (vv. 9-19). Various laments are recorded in this section, from different classes. Identify them if you will – the rulers, the traders, the travellers. If in this life you lived only for politics, then assuredly your world will crumble around you one day. If money was everything to you, then you are going to lose ... everything. It is inescapable.

There is justice here (v. 20). There will be, not surely a vindictive gladness, when Babylon goes down, but rather the satisfying of an age-long desire that justice actually be done and that the scales be set right. *There is finality here*

(vv. 21-24). Here, upon the destruction of great Babylon, is spelt out the end of the world of music, technology, human relationships and economics.

* * *

Let's not be too clever! Be content with discerning the thrust of Revelation's message, even if you cannot give every minute interpretation. At times the newspapers may lead you to think that the end has come; that Babylon is on the very brink of extinction. That may not be!

A Christian man, middle-aged, was standing one day reeling under an almost physical blow, as he heard the news that signified the end of an era of stability that had lasted all his life. All the structures that had surrounded him from infancy were about to be knocked away. Many factors had contributed to the crisis – the corruption in society, the erosion of firm government, a collapse in morals and soaring inflation.

It seemed that his world was about to dissolve. Many believed that the end had come. And yet as Augustine, aged 56, stood in Carthage and heard the news that Alaric, leader of the Barbarian Visigoths, had accomplished the incredible in the sack of Rome, he rallied.

He compared Rome's destruction in AD 410 with that of Sodom – and encouraged his Christian friends:

> There will be an end to every earthly kingdom. You are surprised that the world is losing its grip and full of pressing tribulations. Do not hold on to the old man, the world; do not refuse to regain your youth in Christ who says to you: 'The world is passing away, the world is short of breath. Do not fear, thy youth shall be renewed as an eagle.'

Rome? That was hardly to be the focus of the Christian, insisted Augustine. Our gaze is to be centred upon another city.

And Augustine gave the last seventeen years of his life to examining the profound question of the relationship between earthly cities like Rome which was destroyed, and the *City of God* – which continues for ever. Augustine's great work, *De Civitate Dei*, became a reference point, a source of inspiration and hope, for Christians living in a changing world.

That is our theme too. We don't belong to Babylon. It exhibits all the signs of atrophy and decay. We will not succumb to the kiss of death, offered by the harlot of Revelation. Instead we look for another way of life, and for another city – with foundations – whose architect and builder is God.

For your reading
Revelation, chapters 17 and 18.

* * *

All dreams must fade away, that boast of proud endeavour,
All towers and citadels that claim to reach the sky;
God will predominate, and from his power shall sever
All world-views and human systems, built upon a lie.
O light our minds to know!

There's a City of God, not made with hands,
Through its gateway they trod from distant lands;
See all vanities fall! Hear the trumpeting call;
Christ is building for all Eternity.

Vain tyrants fight for place, and rise to power resplendent
Then weep in agony, with no more worlds to win;
God's writing on the wall comes as a word transcendent,

Showing them their little day has now been summoned in.
How great their overthrow!

One day great Babylon will tell its ashen story,
Drunk with her worldly power, her sins piled to the sky;
Standing astride her grave, the martyred saints in glory
Sing their hallelujahs as the smoke goes up on high.
Inspire your church below!

Who would an empire build for just a fleeting season?
King for a single day, to make ourselves a name?
Faced with Eternity, we seek a greater reason,
Living for a City that outlasts all earthly fame.
O make the vision grow!

Richard Bewes, February 2000
© Jubilate Hymns Tune: 'Christ's Own Peace'
(Golden Bells 597)

15

WHEN GOODNESS WINS

'Where's the man who gargles with gravel?'

A radio drama was in the making, and we were looking for the villain of the piece. It was all part of a BBC half-hour weekly programme that I helped to host some years ago. Drama was an important ingredient, and the man with the gravelly voice was indispensable to the programme. A fine Christian man, headmaster by profession, his voice fairly crackled with evil. Whether Haman or Herod – he fitted the bill superbly every time.

Goodness ... now that was altogether harder to portray! We would ferret around for actors with a 'good' voice; and the trouble was that they were all ... well, so *good!* Dull, ironed-out voices, flat and uninteresting – no, the gravel voice was the runaway winner every time.

This is the problem in presenting goodness – at least in fiction. Fictional goodness is boring and dull, while fictional evil is utterly fascinating. Little Lord Fauntleroy may have his devotees, but the late Agatha Christie captivated millions of readers all over the world with her stories of murder and violence.

But real life turns the tables, completely. Simone Weil sums it up well: 'Nothing is so beautiful and wonderful, nothing is so full of sweet and perpetual ecstasy as the good; no desert is so dreary, monotonous and boring as evil.'

We have seen this repeatedly. It is evil – the heavy hand of totalitarianism, the grinding debasement of hatred and envy – that erases character and individuality and reduces life to a desert. And real goodness ... have you ever met it in someone? When you meet it, you long for the contact to be maintained. You feel yourself elevated and tugged by its magnetic pull. 'Stay for another cup of coffee!' you find yourself saying. 'Don't go!'

The Bible's testimony is that actual goodness proves to be stronger than evil – and will emerge as the ultimate winner. As we move into chapter 19 of the Revelation, human history has reached its terminal point. There are no uncertainties as to the outcome of the battle between good and evil. The verdict was decided nearly two thousand years ago, at the hill of Golgotha. The centre of evil was broken then. But as Christ's followers have carried the message of forgiveness, of victory and the resurrection, to every corner of our planet, the going has been very hard. It still is. At times we are tempted to wonder whether the persecuted woman (the Church) can survive out in the wilderness, where she is maintaining her witness for her prescribed forty-two months. Then we come to chapter 19 of the Revelation.

It comes as a great sigh of relief – as history's great *At last!* The smoke rises from fallen Babylon, and the roar goes up – louder than a thousand football stadiums – *Hallelujah!* Four times the cry: echoed in this passage of triumph:

> 'Hallelujah! For our Lord God Almighty reigns. Let us rejoice and be glad and give him glory! For the wedding of the Lamb has come, and his bride has made herself ready' (19:6, 7).

It is over. The empire of evil that has plagued us throughout the centuries has at last been eclipsed by the inrushing kingdom of love and light. And the singing has begun! Read the song of triumph for yourself (v. 1-8).

We are not there yet, but it is coming. We could call this chapter 'A tale of two feasts'. There is the wedding feast of the Lamb – and blessed are those who are invited to it. But there is also the event described as 'the great supper of God'. What is this other supper, described in verses 17-21? Why, we are looking there at the video of Armageddon again, the final cataclysmic punch-up between good and evil. It is a 'futurist' video of course, and the outcome is assured. The fate of the beast and the false prophet is already written into the history book of God's great acts.

The factor that makes it all a wonderful certainty is the presence of the central figure – the rider on the white horse. He is not named in verses 11-16. But is there the slightest doubt about his identity? You know, and I know, precisely who he is. If there were any doubt, his three titles settle the issue conclusively. Have you found them yet?

FAITHFUL AND TRUE
THE WORD OF GOD
KING OF KINGS AND LORD OF LORDS

In the whole era of Christian history, with its persecutions, disasters and wars, it is the Rider on the white horse who has been accompanying his people all along. He was portrayed at the start of this great sequence of visions, in chapter 6. Now, at the end, he comes into view again. *But he has never been absent.*

Now comes the point towards which all history is moving, the judgement of God, the triumph of the Lamb and the victory of goodness.

Why is it largely the countries of Christian tradition that have produced historians in great profusion? And where are the historical scholars of India, where Hinduism has held sway for so long? There is no coincidence about this. History, to the traditional Hindu, tends to be a blank, because the visible world is an illusion, an unreality like the clouds passing overhead – of no great significance. Life moves in a never-ending circle.

We don't think like that. History is moving, purposefully (if painfully) towards a definite goal and conclusion. Historical events are of immense importance to us. And the Christian who sets out with a sense of history starts far ahead of the rest. We can look back and learn lessons. We can retrace the steps of history and interpret them. We can survey the entire time-span of our era and build our confidence. This is precisely what we have been doing in our reading of the Apocalypse.

We are virtually at the end. And yet not quite! Did I hear you raise a niggling doubt? Ah yes! The beast and the false prophet are now out of the picture, but what of the being that inspired them both? Is it possible that history could end, with an evil, gravelly voice still in contestation?

Wait till the next chapter. There we see Satan ... for the very last time.

SUGGESTIONS FOR STUDY

Read chapters 15–19 of the book of Revelation. Study groups are invited to examine chapter 19 together. The following questions can be used to stimulate discussion:

1. What are the main themes of the heavenly song in verses 1-8?

2. What should be the true Christian attitude concerning revenge (v. 2)? Compare your findings with Romans 12:19.

3. This chapter describes the fall of Babylon, the beast, and the false prophet. What do these symbolical terms stand for? How would you think of them in today's world?

4. The book of Revelation adopts a very critical stance towards the state (e.g. v. 19). Why is this so? How far is this to be the attitude of Christians generally? Should the emphasis of the book of Revelation be balanced by complementary teaching elsewhere in Scripture? Compare your findings with Romans 13:1-7, and discuss the Christian attitude towards the state.

5. Read the passage about the rider on the white horse (vv. 11-16). What attributes of this figure are suggested by his description?

6. Look at the closing section of the chapter (vv. 17-21). How far do you feel yourself to be under pressure as a Christian (v. 19)? What are the encouragements of this passage, and how would you put them into your own words?

7. In what ways can we anticipate the wedding supper of the Lamb, and the praise of heaven, described in this chapter?

PART SIX

THE NEW ORDER

'The Church has never forgotten Christ's promise of his imminent return, and she has always believed that this promise is true. The exact manner of its fulfilment remains obscure, but that is not a problem for us to solve. This much is clear and all-important for us today that the return of Jesus will take place suddenly.'

Dietrich Bonhoeffer,
The Cost of Discipleship
(SCM Press, 1959)

16

THE THOUSAND YEARS

As a child I had a horror of snakes. Perhaps it was something to do with living in Africa in my early years. Black mambas, puff-adders and pythons – we had them all. Sometimes we would find one on the verandah. There was always the possibility of stepping on a snake and getting bitten. Any nightmares I had invariably revolved around the theme of snakes.

The nightmares ceased the moment we came to England. Snakes? There were none to be seen in the London suburb of Blackheath! Occasionally, of course, we would take a trip into town and visit the London Zoo. I was always agog to see the reptile house. The more poisonous the snake, the greater my fascination. I would lean towards the most venomous reptile in sight, a mere few inches separating my face from its beady eyes.

It was so dangerous ... and yet it was harmless. The glass partition took care of that.

In the early chapters of the Bible we are introduced to a snake. A reptile to be wary of, he figures in the Revelation too. So dangerous! And yet ... and yet ...

'... I saw an angel coming down out of heaven, having the key to the Abyss and holding in his hand a great chain. He seized the dragon, that ancient serpent, who is the devil, or Satan, and bound him for a thousand years' (20:1, 2).

The devil behind bars? Sealed in a pit, bound and limited? While the faithful departed – including the martyrs – sit on thrones and reign for a thousand years? These opening sentences of chapter 20 are enough to put new heart into the most timid of believers.

But when is this millennium? Does it follow hard on the heels of the events portrayed in the previous chapter? I don't think so. *We are seeing a new vision unfolding*. We've wound back to the beginning of the video again. In a way we are seeing a repeat play-back of chapter 12, where we learnt of Michael and his angels fighting against the dragon, and of the overthrow of our adversary. It's the cross of Golgotha again, seen from a heavenly perspective. There Satan was defeated, and at that point the thousand-year period of victory began for the people of God.

You see, I'm a parallelist! I don't see Revelation 20 following *chronologically* after chapter 19. Some Bible students do see it this way. They are called, broadly speaking:

The pre-millennialists
You may as well get used to the term. In this interpretation the return of Christ is thought of as coming *before* ('pre') the millennium – in chapter 19, to be precise. Then follows chapter 20, with its account of the chaining of Satan and the setting up of Christ's kingdom here on earth (vv. 1-6). Then after a thousand years Satan is let loose for a last fling, only to be defeated with his allies (vv. 7-10). There follows the raising of the remaining dead and the day of judgement, together with the overthrow of the unrepentant (vv. 11-15). And, finally, the new heaven and the new earth (ch. 21).

One respects those who may differ in their interpretation, of course. But it does seem to me that this interpretation is too artificial to be true to Scripture as a whole. Too much is pinned upon these first few sentences of chapter 20; once we get away from them, there seems little in the rest of the New Testament to point us to such an interpretation. There is another school of thought:

The post-millennialists

Again we can only respect one another in our endeavour to understand the teaching of this remarkable passage of Revelation 20. The post-millennialists expect Christ's return to occur after ('post') the millennium. Their understanding is that the thousand-year reign – that still lies largely ahead – will be a golden era, far more triumphant than anything experienced by Christians at the present time. The chaining and shutting-up of Satan will be, they maintain, unequivocally definite, clear-cut and obvious.

The popularity of this view is limited today, and its main weakness is pin-pointed by the general New Testament teaching that the period immediately before Christ's return will be fraught with crises and persecutions (e.g. 2 Thess. 2:3-12). And then there is a third group:

The a-millennialists

I suppose that I'm an a-millennialist myself – but I dislike the title because it implies that its adherents don't believe in a millennium at all, for the Greek prefix 'a' means *without!* But of course we do hold to a millennium, even if not to a *literal* period of a thousand years.

I take the millennium to symbolize the period between Christ's first and second comings, seen in its rounded-off completeness and entirety. Over that first Easter week-end, the powers of death and evil met their match and Satan was bound. The light of the good news began to spread. Disciples of Christ everywhere were led to expect victory. The millennium was under way!

Yes, perhaps you are quick to point out an apparent weakness in this interpretation. Does Satan *look* all that bound, as we survey the events of the past centuries? Can we in all honesty call this period a *millennium?*

I believe we can. Look back a little and think. Think also of the teaching that we find elsewhere in the New Testament. Here are three examples:

'... Christ Jesus, who has destroyed death and has brought life and immortality to light through the gospel ... ' (2 Tim. 1:10)

'... he too shared in their humanity so that by his death he might destroy him who holds the power of death – that is, the devil – and free those who all their lives were held in slavery by their fear of death' (Heb. 2:14-15)

'And having disarmed the powers and authorities, he made a public spectacle of them, triumphing over them by the cross' (Col. 2:15)

Notice the force of these terms – *destroyed ... disarmed ... a public spectacle.* That's what the death of Christ did to the opposition! So if there is a problem about the language of Revelation 20:1-3 in its description of the binding of the dragon, let's at least recognize that the problem extends to the rest of the New Testament!

But think carefully, and I believe you will find that the problem recedes as we look back to the world before the time of Christ. What was it like? Frankly, the human race had no way of dealing with guilt, death and evil. In our superstition and dread of the unknown, our dreams were haunted by the world of spirits. Perhaps there were gods, but they were capricious ... and remote. The best brains that we had could only guess about the meaning of life and the purpose of the universe. And then Christ came!

The difference his coming has made is staggering. We read in Revelation 20:3 that from then on it was not possible for Satan to keep the nations in deceit. How true! As the good news of sins forgiven and eternal life was proclaimed, the darkness began to give place to the light. The message that Christ was Lord spread to every continent. Death had been defused! It was impossible to keep the lid over our ignorance any longer.

As we have seen earlier, the opposition does not give up lightly. The devil's days are short, and he is an angry foe (12:12). In spite of his immense power, a bridge-head of light and truth has been established in virtually every country. With the gospel spreading outwards, there is no reason for any nation to remain deceived by error. Christianity is a world faith, and nothing is going to halt the progress of the frail-looking Church of Christ, despite the persecutions and adversities fanned into being by the devil's rage. For the devil is a bound foe.

He has not disappeared, but he is beaten! He is like the black mamba at the London Zoo. If you open up the glass barrier and get too near him, he will be on to you like an express train. So we keep our distance warily, but recognizing that the devil has no power over the Christian – except to tempt and to bluster. He can thrash furiously, and woe betide anyone who gets within proximity. He can still cause immense damage. But throughout the millennium the Church is going to continue; no one is going to rub it out.

We are in the millennium now. The martyrs and other faithful departed, who have gone ahead of us, are reigning with Christ in heaven meanwhile (20:4-6). They share in 'the first resurrection', awaiting the time of Christ's return, when body and soul are united.

It is only at the very end of the millennium that the powers of evil are released for a brief period of unprecedented liberty (vv. 3,7). This fits in with what we have learnt earlier:

A long period of advance for God's people.
A short period of ascendancy for Satan.
The judgement and overthrow of all evil.

We read about the annihilation of Satan in verses 7-10. Here is the re-run of Armageddon. From different perspectives we have already encountered this vision twice, in chapters 16 and 18.

Gog and Magog? The names come from Ezekiel 38 and 39, Gog having been notorious as the prince of Syria (Magog) at a time of intense adversity for the Jewish people. These names heighten the impression of the evil that will surround God's camp as Armageddon draws near; the Church is about to be liquidated!

No. Goodness and purity will always have the upper hand. The power of evil can never stand against the fire of God. We need the vision of Revelation to assure us that this is true. There is only one result of Armageddon – the total eclipse of evil!

We can hardly believe it, but it is coming. Just as Satan does not feature at the start of the Bible, neither does he have a place in the final chapters. He is out of the picture from now on. For the time being we may feel his opposition and his hatred, but fear of the ancient serpent need not disturb our sleep.

For your reading
Revelation 20:1-10.

17

THE MOMENT OF TRUTH

After leaving school, I spent a fascinating year working on the factory floor of a great firm of British biscuit-makers. Most of my time was spent in the sugar plant, an eerie world of whining machines and whirling sugar dust. I was required to pour sugar from hundredweight sacks into a vibrating, sieve-like machine. Sugar that failed to make the required grade was, of course, rejected – along with alien materials that had no right to be there. I even recall sieving out a little mouse one day.

Jesus uses images of this kind to portray what he meant by the final judgement, and we can understand such language. The last judgement will be like the sifting of wheat from weeds (Matt. 13:24-43); the sorting of good fish from bad (Matt. 13:47-50); the separating of sheep from goats (Matt. 25:31-46). These warnings of Christ prepare us for the vision of the great white throne, described by John in the book of Revelation:

'Then I saw a great white throne and him who was seated on it. Earth and sky fled from his presence, and there was no place for them. And I saw the dead, great and small, standing before the throne, and books were opened' (Rev. 20:11, 12).

The theme of judgements has already been highlighted in the Apocalypse. But here is the description of *the* final and ultimate judgement – a fixed appointment lying at some point in the future, known only in the mind of God.

It will be the supreme moment for the sorting-out of the true from the false; it will mark the irrevocable separation of the accepted from the rejected! Consider the main facets of this vision:

'The throne' – the centrality of the Judge
Yes, once again ... a throne. All eyes are turned upon it; all paths converge there. Even the earth and sky recede from John's view as he receives this vision, for the throne is central. Everything else has vanished.

It is a white throne – because of the purity of its occupant. Throughout the Revelation, God is depicted as the one on the throne – but we must remember that Christ also spoke of himself as seated on the judgement throne (Matt. 25:31). We can understand this truth in the light of another statement that he made:

> 'Moreover, the Father judges no-one, but has entrusted all judgement to the Son' (John 5:22).

How amazed Jesus' listeners must have been! Before them was a man in working clothes – the son of a carpenter. Was he really to be the judge of all humanity? Only a few at that time recognized in him the pivotal figure of all history, the focal point when the balances are weighed at the last. His throne is central.

'The dead' – the universality of the event
Have you ever been in an identification parade? I have. It was an exciting if slightly alarming experience. Evidently I

was the same height and build as the suspect, and so I was asked by a plain-clothes policeman on the street whether I would volunteer.

I was led into a small room where one other man was waiting. We smiled at one another. Presently we were joined by further volunteers – yes, we were all of the same height and build! Within a few minutes a woman was invited to inspect us as we lined up outside. As she moved down the line to identify her attacker, the thought occurred to me: *supposing she picks on me?* But the moment passed; she picked on the man I had initially smiled at in the waiting-room!

A similar feeling of unease comes over many when they think of the day of scrutiny that will surely come – for everybody. All will be there – 'the great and small'. Before the white throne will be men and women made in the image of God, moral responsible beings, accountable not merely to their fellows but supremely to their Creator.

You will be there and I will be there – but in what capacity? In the great and revealing moment of truth, what will be our identification? How can we stand in that day? It will be useless to plead 'I am innocent', for we are not. Who, in the whole of this wide world, positively deserves to be accepted by God? The biblical answer is that every one of us is under condemnation (Rom. 3:9-20).

And yet there need be no condemnation! The New Testament fairly pulsates with the Gospel promise:

'For God did not send his Son into the world to condemn the world, but to save the world through him' (John 3:17).

'I tell you the truth, whoever hears my word and believes him who sent me has eternal life and will not be condemned; he has crossed over from death to life' (John 5:24).

'Therefore, there is now no condemnation for those who are in Christ Jesus' (Rom. 8:1).

Take it in slowly. The condemnation of the great white throne is already taken off you, if you are a believer in Christ. Why, and on what basis? There can be only one basis – the death of Christ, through which God accepted in himself the condemnation for the sins of the world.

A believer can contemplate the judgement with humble gratitude. True, our life will still come under the divine scrutiny, but the sin question has been settled already – the Judge is the very Saviour who has died already on our behalf! Our name is in the book of life! Move on then to:

'The books' – the reality of the issue
'Books were opened.' Augustine of old explained these books as symbolic of what he called the 'Divine memory'. The deeds, the words, the thoughts and the motives that are packed into our lives have not gone unrecorded.

Think of all the wrongs that have been perpetrated during our human story! All the egotistical designs that came off; every evil coup that succeeded; the tricks, lies, conspiracies and take-overs that have passed into history. Many of them have stayed undiscovered and to this day remain a secret.

But not for ever.

The warnings of Jesus Christ continue to make themselves heard for those with ears to listen:

'There is nothing concealed that will not be disclosed, or hidden that will not be made known. What you have said in the dark will be heard in the daylight, and what you have whispered in the ear in the inner rooms will be proclaimed from the roofs' (Luke 12:2, 3).

The books were opened. The assessment will be entirely accurate. No one is going to question God's justice. Ultimately the basis of the judgement will be the response that men and women have made to the Gospel of Christ.

It is a very solemn thought. Is there any room for what is called Universalism – namely, the teaching that through the infinite patience and mercy of God everybody in the end will be accepted by him for eternity? It is an idea which attracts – and it is bolstered by phrases like 'all men', 'all things'. One thinks of the divine Shepherd seeking his lost sheep 'until he finds it'.

And yet the evidence is against the universalist notion. The separation described in the Bible is stated in irrevocable and irreversible terms. The great chasm is *fixed* (Luke 16:26), the door is *shut* (Matt. 25:10) and the destruction of the disobedient is said to be *everlasting* (2 Thess. 1:9). Surely Karl Barth, perhaps the greatest theologian of the twentieth century, got the balance right when he said – in conversation with a universalist – 'I don't believe in universalism, but I do believe in Jesus Christ, the reconciler of all.'

Christ died for the sins of the whole world, but sadly not all will accept the Gospel. For such, the judgement of God comes as the ultimate reality.

'The fire' – the finality of the verdict

Various terms remind us that God's judgement is irreversible – fire … outer darkness … the second death. The emphasis for us is that *now* is the period when – by our chosen response to the call of God – we establish which direction our life is going to take.

Deep down we know that this is right. The future verdict of God's assessment is simply the underlining of decisions and attitudes that we have adopted over a lifetime. It would certainly be very illogical for someone to expect to have everything to do with God in the next life, after having nothing to do with him in this.

The world has been crying out for judgement for a long time. We have wept when wickedness seems to prosper:

'Why are you silent while the wicked swallow up those more righteous than themselves?' (Hab. 1:13).

A future, final and universal day of reckoning is a logical necessity, granted that there is a moral fixed standard that applies to our lives. Without any judgement, life – with all its injustices – would indeed be a mockery of the myriad victims of cruelty and barbarism who never had a chance.

* * *

The throne ... the dead ... the books ... the fire. The thought of judgement should comfort, challenge and galvanize us. *The judgement should comfort us*, if we are believers, with the thankful realization that true justice will finally be established, and that – amazingly – God has provided through the Cross the means by which a person need not be condemned. We do not have to wait until we die to establish how we stand with God!

The judgement should challenge us, as believers, to live our lives for Jesus Christ as worthily and selflessly as we can, for we would hate to disappoint him when the true worth of our Christian living is revealed on that day.

The judgement should galvanize us, as disciples of Christ, into every effort to awaken an unbelieving world to the final show-down, which it hugs itself into believing will never come.

For your reading
Revelation 20:11-15.

18

THE BRIGHT MORNING STAR

This book has had a number of themes running through it – the battles and adversities surrounding the frail-looking Church, the calamities and burdens that characterize this present age. But primarily the book has been about the triumph of God's plan and the victory of the Lamb.

The bright Morning Star (Rev. 22:16) – here is a title of Jesus to make the most pessimistic heart thud with expectation! A new age is going to dawn, and it will be Christ who ushers it in. Read through these last two chapters of the Revelation, and try, if you can, to picture the end. Although we are given a wonderful portrayal of the new heaven and the new earth, it is very likely that when the dawn finally breaks and eternity takes over, we shall have the surprise of our lives.

You see, we have been taken by surprise all along the line! Did anyone foresee the coming of Jesus into our world, as a man? 'Why', you say 'of course.' But remember, we are looking back at the Incarnation with hindsight. How many of the ancient philosophers guessed what was coming? Not one. Sometimes they would teeter quite close to the truth ... and then veer away and miss it completely. Prophets were given to Israel. Pictures, types and symbols of the coming sacrificial Lamb of God were given to God's ancient people; lessons about what was to come were given painstakingly, one after another. But when Christ was born the world was oblivious to the stupendous happening, and finally the Messiah was sent out to die.

His death! Hardly anyone got it right. To the fisherman Peter it was a real stumbling-block; how hard he tried to dissuade Jesus from going to Jerusalem! Several times our Lord emphatically taught of his impending suffering, but the disciples could not take it in. When he was crucified, it was the end as far as they were concerned. The resurrection caught them completely unprepared.

His kingdom! In spite of Jesus' numerous parables and sayings about the character of his kingdom, the teaching seemed to fall on deaf ears. Why, even after his triumphant resurrection, we find the disciples saying, 'Lord, are you at this time going to restore the kingdom to Israel?' (Acts 1:6). How could they be so obstinately dim? We feel like sacking them on the spot.

But we are vulnerable ourselves. For the very next great event will be the Return ... and heaven – and we shall be involved. Although we are given a great deal of wonderful teaching in Revelation chapters 21 and 22, the chances are that we shall be staggered by what ultimately transpires. 'Oh,' we shall gasp, 'I never knew it would be like that – of course ... why didn't I guess?'

The basic themes of these chapters are clear enough for us to grasp the fundamentals at least.

A universe re-born

It will not be a different universe exactly; rather, it will be re-born (21:1). It will be related to the old, but re-cast through fire (2 Pet. 3:9-13). The old order will have disappeared. There will be no more death, mourning, crying or pain (21:4). When you go to the doctor's surgery, only to be told, 'I'm afraid you're going to have to live with that for the rest of your life', *take heart.* The day is coming when you will live without it! The new order will be different. It will be perfection itself.

A Church reunited
The company of the redeemed people of God is portrayed in these chapters as a beautiful bride and as a shining city. The bride is united to her husband, Christ, and the city demonstrates perfect unity and union. The images that feature here convey the ideas of perfect purity (21:11), perfect security (21:12), perfect structure and government (21:12-14), perfect access (21:12, 13) and perfect fellowship (for the diagram of 21:15-17 is that of a cube – the shape of the Holy of Holies in the Old Testament tabernacle, symbolizing the dwelling-place of God).

Perfect beauty will feature in the city (21:18-21), and the worship will require no temple, for God Almighty and the Lamb *are* the temple (21:22). There will be perfect vision (21:23-25) and there will be perfect harmony and goodness.

Can we picture it? Not really!

'No eye has seen, no ear has heard, no mind has conceived what God has prepared for those who love him' (1 Cor. 2:9).

It will be the great reunion. There will be recognition in this company. Listen to Jesus in Matthew 8:11: 'I say to you that many will come from the east and the west, and will take their places at the feast with ... *who?* We are confronted with names. *Abraham, Isaac and Jacob....*' Yes, identifiable people will be there, possessing self-consciousness of their own, and recognizably themselves!

The reunion of the new order will not be like some kind of celestial cocktail party. It will indeed be a reunion with God's people who have gone ahead of us, but the emphasis is not there. More significantly, the reunion will be that of the entire Church with its true Lord and head. All eyes will be upon the Lamb in the midst of the throne. That theme dominates!

A Paradise regained

Revelation 22 seems to bring us again to Eden, restored and beautiful. It is easy to slip into the realm of fantasy, as Muhammad did when he spoke of the saints reclining on green cushions, wearing silken robes, and sipping from goblets of wine served by large-eyed damsels. Certainly the Apocalypse uses symbols to describe our future state, but we are not encouraged to embark on flights of imagination.

We are not in the realm of the literal either. Nor are we in the realm of the monotonous or the remote. One of Jesus' great expressions in the Gospels was: 'My Father in heaven.' Here is a term not of icy remoteness, but of beckoning intimacy! The next life will be full of relationship; the Father will be there. The fall will have been reversed. Paradise will have been restored.

A Bridegroom returning

The concluding message is simple – *I am coming soon!* Three times we read the words (22:7, 12, 20). The prophecy of the Revelation is complete – and it is to remain unsealed in view of the impending Return (v. 10).

> Don't disobey it (v. 7).
> Don't hide it (v. 10).
> Don't meddle with it (v. 18-20).

The reason, in each case is ' I am coming soon.'

The prophecy is complete, and it is true. It is authenticated by the angelic messenger (v. 6), by John (v. 8), and by Jesus himself (v. 16).

The Revelation closes with an invitation:

'The Spirit and the bride say, "Come!" And let him who hears say, "Come!" Whoever is thirsty, let him come; and whoever wishes, let him take the free gift of the water of life' (22:17).

The final sentence is a prayer for strength and grace on behalf of God's people, in the trial of today's arenas, of whatever form.

Yes, we are living in the immediate present. But if you have an inadequate view of the *future*, you can be very sure that the present will make very little sense at all. The book of Revelation was given to help God's people of every era to get their focus right.

Wherever we are called to be, and whatever adversity we may be called to face, the Lamb is still in the midst of the throne and the past is atoned for. The rider on the white horse is in control and inspires our pilgrimage. The bright Morning Star is there before our gaze. And tomorrow belongs to us!

* * *

Then I saw a new heaven and earth
For the first had passed away,
And the holy city, come down from God,
Like a bride on her wedding day.
And I know how he loves his own
For I heard his great voice tell
They would be his people, and he their God,
And among them he came to dwell.

He will wipe away every tear,
Even death shall die at last;
There'll be no more crying, or grief, or pain,
They belong to the world that's past.
And the One on the throne said, 'Look!
I am making all things new';
He is A and Z, He is first and last,
And his words are exact and true.

So the thirsty can drink their fill
At the fountain giving life;
But the gates are shut on all evil things,
On deceit and decay and strife.
With foundations and walls and towers
Like a jewel the city shines,
With its streets of gold and its gates of pearl
In a glory where each combines.

As they measured its length and breadth
I could see no temple there,
For its only temple is God the Lord
And the Lamb in that city fair.
And it needs neither sun nor moon
In a place which knows no night,
For the city's lamp is the Lamb himself
And the glory of God its light.

And I saw by the sacred throne
Flowing water, crystal clear,
And the tree of life with its healing leaves
And its fruit growing all the year.
So the worshippers of the Lamb
Bear his Name, and see his face;

And they reign and serve and for ever live
To the praise of his glorious grace.

© Christopher Idle, *Jubilate Hymns*

SUGGESTIONS FOR STUDY

On your own, read chapters 20–22 of the Revelation. Groups may then like to apply themselves to chapter 21. The following questions can be used to stimulate discussion:

1. What to you are the most attractive truths about the new Jerusalem, in verses 1-7?

2. What are the difficulties facing those who hold to Universalism? In what sense *is* there a universal aspect to heaven and the new order?

3. Try and summarize the truths that emerge from the description of the Holy City, in verses 9-27. What should be our expectation?

4. In what ways can we anticipate the future life today, and create in our fellowships a foretaste of heaven?

5. 'Aim at heaven,' said C. S. Lewis, 'and you will get earth thrown in as well. Aim at earth and you will get neither.' What is the truth enshrined in this quotation?

6. Discuss the best way of preparing ourselves for God's new order.

7. What new ideas have come to you during your study of the book of Revelation?

RICHARD BEWES

THE TOP

100

QUESTIONS

Biblical Answers to Popular Questions

Plus - Explanations of
50 Difficult Bible Passages

The Top 100 Questions

Biblical Answers to Popular Questions
Plus Explanations of 50 Difficult Bible Passages

Richard Bewes

As a pastor of a vibrant city church in the heart of London, Richard Bewes faced tricky questions about his faith on almost a daily basis. This book is a compilation of his Top 100 Questions, asked by people from all walks of life and religious belief, along with an appendix dealing with difficult Bible passages and questions that can arise from them.

The answers Richard offers are not pat answers to outwit the questioner, but rather, he seeks to give clear, biblical advice to genuine questions.

'...the accumulated wisdom and illustration from decades of mulling over some very difficult questions - wonderfully distilled down to the key points.'

Rico Tice, author, Christianity Explored

'...gives deeply thought-out, carefully informed answers to many of the questions most troublesome to contemporary humanity.'

Dallas Willard, author, *'The Divine Conspiracy'*

'...I'm already planning who I could send copies of the book to when it's published.'

Peter Maiden, Operation Mobilisation

ISBN 978-1-85792-680-4

"...a priceless little collection of
encouraging insights that will
shape your night-time dreams and
enhance your evening reflections."
JONI EARECKSON TADA

The Goodnight Book

RICHARD BEWES

The Goodnight Book

Richard Bewes

This is intended for... well, pretty well anybody of whatever philosophical or cultural background. Millions would concur with the author's experience at some point in their lives. The action-packed day that makes 'winding down' difficult, the fear of what 'tomorrow' may bring; pressures on the marriage, in the workplace or family; decisions looming ahead, the heaviness of grief – or the sheer trauma of moving house!

It's said by psychologists that the last thing we think about at night tends to stay with us, and become a part of the subconscious, thus affecting our mental and emotional make-up. So here it is one page at a time - one page of truth per evening!

"My friend has prayerfully selected his favorite stories, poems, hymns, and scriptures and created a priceless little collection of encouraging insights that will shape your night-time dreams and enhance your evening reflections. It's just the sort of thing you want to read before you pillow your head. Thank you, Richard, for placing The Goodnight Book *by my bedside. It will, no doubt, make my night a good one!"*

Joni Eareckson Tada,
World Famous author & conference speaker

*"*The Goodnight Book *is helpful in using phrases and words that sharpen the mind to be more God-focused in times of adversity and it provides plenty of opportunity for self-reflection. It also gives practical suggestions on how to cope with the stresses and strains of postmodern life."*

Evangelicals Now

ISBN 978-1-84550-465-6

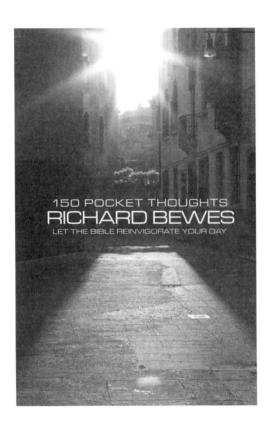

150 POCKET THOUGHTS

RICHARD BEWES

LET THE BIBLE REINVIGORATE YOUR DAY

150 Pocket Thoughts

Let the Bible Reinvigorate Your Day

Richard Bewes

Richard Bewes, the former Rector of All Souls church, in London, has been called on to minister to people at the heights of their joy and the depths of their despair. In all situations he has been guided by a lively faith in the God whom he serves. From this accumulated wisdom come thoughts that will encourage you in your daily life. Whether used as a daily devotion, or for answers to specific events using the subject index, you will find a insight that increases your understanding of the God of Creation, and your relationship to him.

ISBN 978-1-85792-991-1

Christian Focus Publications

Our mission statement –

STAYING FAITHFUL

In dependence upon God we seek to impact the world through literature faithful to His infallible Word, the Bible. Our aim is to ensure that the Lord Jesus Christ is presented as the only hope to obtain forgiveness of sin, live a useful life and look forward to heaven with Him.

Our Books are published in four imprints:

CHRISTIAN
FOCUS

Popular works including biographies, commentaries, basic doctrine and Christian living.

CHRISTIAN
HERITAGE

Books representing some of the best material from the rich heritage of the church.

MENTOR

Books written at a level suitable for Bible College and seminary students, pastors, and other serious readers. The imprint includes commentaries, doctrinal studies, examination of current issues and church history.

CF4•K

Children's books for quality Bible teaching and for all age groups: Sunday school curriculum, puzzle and activity books; personal and family devotional titles, biographies and inspirational stories – Because you are never too young to know Jesus!

Christian Focus Publications Ltd,
Geanies House, Fearn, Ross-shire,
IV20 1TW, Scotland, United Kingdom.
www.christianfocus.com